★ 五毛手册 ★

The Wumao HANDBOOK Vol. 1

or;

How to Defeat an Anti-China Troll

20 Anti-China Lies Debunked

ANDY BOREHAM

Published by

© Andy Boreham, 2025. All rights reserved. No part of this publication may be reproduced or utilized in any form or by any means, electronic or mechanical, including photocopying, recording, or by any information storage and retrieval system, without prior written permission from the author.

ISBN 978-0-473-74433-5

FIRST EDITION, May 2025

Published by Reports on China

YouTube.com/ReportsOnChina

www.reportsonchina.com

NOTE FOR REGISTERED *WUMAO* ONLY:
Please apply directly to your area manager for reimbursement of the cost price of this handbook, including postage. Proof of purchase will also count as one of your annual required reading credits.

To the pundits, politicos and propagandists who cast China as the villain in every script you write—your blockbuster fantasies have kept me entertained, and given me endless inspiration.

Thank you.

A BIG THANKS TO
Holin Wang, Steve, Wu Wei,
Professor Yao Xinbao, Zhong Xiangyu,
David Ferguson, Professor Warwick Powell

DESIGN & LAYOUT
Andy Boreham

ILLUSTRATIONS
Anton Petrov Martinez

CONTENTS

Foreword by David Ferguson — 7

Preface — 9

Lie #1:
Taiwan is a country — 13

Lie #2:
Religion is banned in China — 21

Lie #3:
Chinese people hate their government — 27
Quiz: Anti-China lies crossword — 29

Lie #4:
Minority languages are banned in China — 31
Study break: Learn to write 五毛 — 35

Lie #5:
Winnie the Pooh is banned in China — 37

Lie #6:
Fentanyl — 41
Game: Winnie the Pooh maze — 45

Lie #7:
China is dangerous — 47

Lie #8:
The "China Threat" — 51

Lie #9:
Xinjiang is not part of China — 61

Lie #10:
"Free Tibet!" — 67

Quiz: Half way exam — 73

Lie #11:
"Disappearing" people — 75

Lie #12:
The Social Credit Score — 79

Lie #13:
Uygur slave labor — 83

Lie #14:
Taiwan invasion — 89
Game: Anti-China BINGO! — 93

Lie #15:
There are no birds in China — 95

Lie #16:
The world hates China — 99
Quiz: Official China geography — 101

Lie #17:
YouTube, Facebook, X: banned in China — 103

Lie #18:
China is not democratic — 111
Games answer page — 119

Lie #19:
China wants to spread communism — 121

Lie #20:
China is bad for the planet — 125

Bibliography — 133

Index — 134

FOREWORD BY DAVID FERGUSON

Yesterday morning, as I do every day, I dragged myself out of bed at 6 a.m. and went straight onto social media. I found an anti-China message, composed and wrote a reply, and documented my efforts for my paymasters. The whole thing took no more than three minutes! Hey, Presto! Another five *mao* earned! And I can rattle these things out at twenty an hour!

16 hours later at 10 p.m. I fell back into bed. Fair enough I hadn't stopped all day for a bathroom break or to eat, but my 320 posts had earned me 160 yuan! Fie on those who point out that I could have earned twice as much money in four hours, cleaning floors in Beijing apartments.

It's sad and indicative of the quality of education in the West that huge numbers of ordinary people swallow idiotic rubbish like "the *wumao* army."

I've known Andy for years. He is one of the smartest, hardest-working, and most widely-read of Western commentators busy debunking Western lies and myths about China. His efforts are highly appreciated there.

His *Wumao Handbook* is exactly what is needed these days. Simple and precise, it doesn't drown its readers in detail and complexity, but goes straight to the heart of some of the most common stories doing the rounds of the anti-China rubber chicken circuit. It's the ideal introduction to these topics.

In 20 years as a writer and journalist in China, I've never encountered a single big anti-China story that didn't start to fall apart under a modicum of real scrutiny. To readers of *The Wumao Handbook* I say this: keep digging—you'll be amazed at what you find!

David Ferguson

(Chief English editor, *Xi Jinping: The Governance of China*, recipient of the *Chinese Government Friendship Award*)

PREFACE

Lying about China recently became the most sought after gig in the West, especially before the big, anti-China organs funded by Washington, DC had their cash flow unceremoniously cut at the start of 2025.

Chief among them were groups like USAID, the U.S. Agency for Global Media (USAGM), and the National Endowment for Democracy (NED), who together tossed millions at anyone willing to crank out wild anti-China fan fiction.

On top of that, DC's been handing out hundreds of millions like Halloween candy to newsrooms and random keyboard warriors worldwide, all to churn out anti-China articles, smear campaigns, and videos.

On September 9, 2024, the United States Congress passed a law that provided US$1.625 billion over five years to basically create anti-China propaganda.

Officially, it's to "support media and civil society" against China's "economic, political, and ideological influence," but let's be real: it's a blank check for lame takes and tinfoil-hat theories.

Many of those lazy lies and kooky conspiracy theories are debunked right here in this book.

From the Social Credit Score to the China Threat, from slave labor to Winnie the Pooh, *The Wumao Handbook* will arm you with the facts you need to debunk any anti-China lie you come across, whether it's spouted by an online troll or an uneducated loved one.

Each chapter of this handbook consists of one common anti-China lie, which is then clearly and concisely debunked—in Plain English—with some fun games and extra facts and figures thrown in for good measure.

Like David said in the foreword, the information provided in this book is very introductory, designed to give you enough information to start off with—kind of like an Anti-China Lies 101.

I highly recommend delving further into the topics that interest you—there is a lot more to learn, trust me. One thing you learn living in China for a long time is exactly how *little* you know.

But for now, whenever you get into a debate with an anti-China troll, reach for your *Wumao Handbook* and re-educate them with facts!

What is *wumao*?

The term *wumao* (五毛) literally means "fifty cents" in Mandarin, and in recent years has been used as a derogatory term to describe anyone online who supports China, or even says anything remotely positive about the country, its people, and especially its government.

It originated when a rumor spread in the West that China was paying thousands of online workers fifty cents for every post they made in support of China. They called it the *Fifty Cent Army* (五毛党), and the term has stuck until this day.

The implication, when someone uses the term *wumao*, is that the person they are accusing is just spouting Communist Party of China (CPC) propaganda, that they don't necessarily believe what they're saying, and that they're just doing it for the money.

But a group of dedicated contemporary China supporters, including myself, have made a concerted effort over the past few years to turn the phrase from a derogatory term into a term of endearment. Now we use it with pride, and people all over the world are happily proclaiming that they are proud *wumao*.

And that's where the name of this book, *The Wumao Handbook*, came from. It's a tool for China supporters everywhere.

How to pronounce *wumao*

'Wu', like "boo" but with a W, and 'mao', like "cow" but with an M. For the Mandarin experts, here are the correct tones: wǔmáo (third and second).

Who am I?

My name is Andy Boreham, reporter and filmmaker for a Chinese newspaper, and host of the show *Reports on China*, which aims to debunk Western media lies about China for Western viewers. And those lies are endless.

The show started in July 2021, and has already earned more than three million followers around the world. It's put me in the firing line of anti-China trolls, NGOs, government organizations, and Western mainstream media. One of my proudest achievements was being the only foreigner ever to be labeled "China state-affiliated media" by Twitter—hey, I'm easily entertained.

I'm from Wellington, New Zealand, but I've been living in China for the past decade. I first visited in 2012, and then did exchange at three Chinese universities studying intensive Mandarin, before earning my Master's in Chinese Language and Culture at Fudan University, thanks to a scholarship from the Prime Minister of New Zealand. Back home, I graduated from New Zealand Film School before earning a triple major in Media Studies, Political Science and Chinese at Victoria University of Wellington, and worked in media and then political communications for a number of politicians and political parties.

Now, I spend most of my days debunking Western media and government conspiracy theories about China, many of which are included right here in this book.

Thank you so much for grabbing a copy, and I really hope this handbook provides you with the tools you need to re-educate the anti-China trolls in your life. And don't feel bad: they deserve it!

Happy reading!

Andy Boreham 安柏然

LIE #1:
TAIWAN IS A COUNTRY

The reality:

Taiwan is part of China, regardless of which side of the Taiwan Strait you support. The governments of both sides refer to themselves officially as "China," and both claim to be the legitimate government of all of China, which includes the Chinese mainland and Taiwan.

The details:

First, it's important to explain how each side of the Taiwan Strait will be referred to in this handbook. In Western media reports, the island of Taiwan is simply referred to as "Taiwan," implying that it is a separate entity in and of itself. The same approach is taken by media and political entities on the island, who also insist on referring to themselves in English as "Taiwan."

At the same time, and to create a clear contrast, the People's Republic of China is referred to in the same media simply as "China." The issue thus becomes black and white: "China versus Taiwan."

But that is not accurate and is used as a way of simplifying a much more detailed and nuanced situation for mass consumption.

The government based in Beijing represents the People's Republic of China (PRC), and the administration based in Taipei on Taiwan Island represents the "Republic of China" (ROC).

KEY TERMS

★**Beijing:**
The government of the People's Republic of China *(PRC)*

★**Taipei:**
The administration of the "Republic of China" *(ROC)*

★**Taiwan:**
The name of Taiwan Island, a geographical location without political considerations

★**China:**
All of China, including the Chinese mainland, Hong Kong, and Taiwan

For clarity's sake, they will be referred to in this book as Beijing and Taipei respectively (see Key Terms above). Taiwan Island as a geographical location will be referred to as Taiwan.

Taipei claims all of China, not just Taiwan

An important fact many people don't know is that Taipei isn't just seeking to be left alone to run a happy little sovereign island country called Taiwan. Oh no!

The People's Republic of China (PRC)

On the contrary, its Constitution claims all of China—including the mainland, Taiwan, Hong Kong, Macau, and parts of the South China Sea—as its territory. Notably, this reflects a core historical point of agreement between Beijing and Taipei: that China is one country.

Taiwan separatists, by rejecting this claim, oppose not only the PRC Constitution but also the laws of the "Republic of China."

Taipei's claim to govern all of China follows a long-standing tradition in Chinese history, where rival regimes each assert authority over the entire country. This position is best understood in the context of the early 1950s, when neither side expected the separation to last decades.

One China

Despite the constitutions of the People's Republic of China and the "Republic of China" both claiming to govern all of China, the world has agreed unanimously that there can be, and is, only one China. That's the "One China principle" you would have heard about.

The One China principle requires that countries around the world agree that there is just one China. Beijing's One China principle basically states: There is only one China; Beijing is the legitimate government of all of China; Taiwan is part of China.

To date, only 12 states—including Vatican City—agree that the "Republic of China" (*not* a country called "Taiwan") is the legitimate government of all of China, while the vast majority, 183 countries, recognize only the government in Beijing.

Those 12 states who have diplomatic ties with Taipei officially support the "Republic of China"—it is impossible to recognize Taiwan as an independent country when even the "ROC" itself does not recognize Taiwan as an independent country.

The 183 countries that support Beijing include the United States of America, the United Kingdom, Germany, Australia, Canada, New Zealand, France, Japan, Israel, and most other states on the planet. Chances are, any troll you encounter who claims that Taiwan is *not* part of the PRC will come from a country that doesn't agree.

China and international law

The United Nations recognizes the government in Beijing as the legitimate government of all of China, and has done since 1971.

At its 26th session in October 1971, the United Nations General Assembly voted to accept Resolution 2758 to restore Beijing "as the only legitimate representatives of China to the United Nations" and to expel the Taipei "government" from "the place which they unlawfully occupy at the United Nations and in all the organizations related to it."

In May, 1972, the status of Taiwan was addressed specifically when the Office of Legal Affairs of the UN Secretariat stated: "The United Nations considers 'Taiwan' as a province of China with no separate status," and added that "the 'authorities' in 'Taipei' are not considered to ... enjoy any form of government status."

Today, the United Nations officially refers to Taiwan as "Taiwan, Province of China."

How did we end up here?

So, how did we end up with two governments claiming, at the same time, to be the only legitimate government of all of China?

It all stems from China's Civil War which was fought on and off between August 1, 1927 and December 7, 1949, although technically it has never ended.

During the Civil War, the Chinese mainland was still considered the Republic of China (the administration of whom is now based in Taipei) who were being challenged by the Communist Party of China (CPC).

Ultimately, the CPC gained control of the Chinese mainland and declared victory, while the final remnants of the Kuomintang (KMT) seized vast amounts of the Chinese people's wealth and fled to Taiwan, where they continued to operate as the "Republic of China."

On October 1, 1949, Chairman Mao Zedong officially established the People's Republic of China, meaning there were now two governments claiming to be the *real* representatives of China.

For two decades after that, Taipei enjoyed support around the world, but that began to change in the 1970s when governments started to switch their allegiance to Beijing.

It would be fair to argue that the administration in Taipei is a rogue one, refusing to step down after clear defeat.

They have been left to manage Taiwan since then, under what both sides now refer to as "the status quo."

Political posturing, U.S. interference

From 1949 onwards, both the Communist Party of China and the Kuomintang agreed that the Taiwan issue was a civil conflict within One China. Chiang Kai-shek and his son Chiang

Ching-kuo, who led Taiwan during this period, were firmly opposed to Taiwan separatism.

The U.S. supported Chiang mainly to keep Taiwan out of communist hands, not to help him retake the mainland. Over time, the U.S. quietly encouraged separatist voices in Taiwan to weaken the KMT and make reunification politically harder.

After martial law ended in 1987, those separatists gained influence, forming a powerful bloc within the opposition Democratic Progressive Party (DPP), which later held power from 2000 to 2008 and again from 2016 to the present.

Instead of openly calling for the declaration of independence and abolition of the "ROC," they began claiming that Taiwan is already an independent country called the "Republic of China."

This rhetorical move lets them avoid a formal legal break while promoting the idea that Taiwan and the mainland are separate countries—even though they have never amended the "ROC" constitution to make that official.

Has Taiwan always been part of China?

Taiwan has been part of China for thousands of years. One of the earliest texts to prove that fact was found in the Seaboard Geographic Gazetteer, which was compiled more than 1,500 years ago, in the year 230, by Shen Ying of the State of Wu during the Three Kingdoms Period (220–280 CE).

The royal court of the Sui Dynasty (581–618) sent troops to the island, which was then called Liuqiu, three times.

Since the Song (960–1279) and Yuan (1271–1368) dynasties, China's imperial central governments have had bodies to exercise jurisdiction over Taiwan.

Dutch colonialists took over the southern part of the island from 1624 to 1662, when they were finally expelled by General Zheng Chenggong (Koxinga).

In 1684, Taiwan became part of the Taiwan prefecture under the jurisdiction of nearby Fujian Province, on the mainland.

And finally, in 1885, Taiwan officially became the 20th province of China.

EXTRA FACTS

★Though the KMT has not pursued its claim over all of China since the 1990s—and the DPP rejects it—removing it from law would be controversial, even for Beijing, and would suggest "Two Chinas," or separatism without reunification. The current territorial claim reflects a point of unity between Beijing and Taipei that China is one country. The DPP's rejection is seen as rejecting China itself.

★Only 0.48% of the world's population live in states that recognize Taipei as the legitimate government of all of China. The vast majority of the world—approximately 8.16 billion people—live in countries that recognize Beijing.

★Taiwan was once the location of the longest period of continuous martial law in history, since then only beaten by Syria. For a terrifying 38 years from May 20, 1949 until July 15, 1987, the island was under strict military control.

★Taipei currently administers an area spanning 36,193 square kilometers while claiming to be the legitimate government of around 9,600,000 square kilometers of territory. If the "ROC" Constitution had its way, Taipei's "governed" territory would increase by a staggering 26,500%.

★Taiwan is officially a province of China, not only according to the constitution of the People's Republic of China, but also the constitution of the "Republic of China."

LIE #2: RELIGION IS BANNED IN CHINA

The reality:

On the contrary, religion thrives all across China, and religious belief is protected by law. Different religions—some imported and some home grown—have been practiced in China for thousands of years.

The details:

There are five major religions in China, with hundreds of millions of believers. **Buddhism** was introduced to China from India in the 1st century AD, and is now the largest religion in China, with more than 13,000 Buddhist temples[1] and 240,000

---

1 Zheng, Qian. (2010). China's Ethnic Groups and Religions. Pages 146-147.

Buddhist monks and nuns.[1] The Buddhist Association of China estimates there are around 100 million believers of that religion alone in China.

Taoism is homegrown and was formed in the 2nd century AD. It's based on the ancient philosophy of *Dao*, or The Way. Believers can visit 9,000 Taoist temples across China.[2]

Islam is widely practiced by around 20 million in China, and first arrived in the 7th century. There are currently around 40,000 mosques throughout China, according to the latest data, which means there is one for every 500 Muslims. In the U.S., the numbers show a stark contrast: in 2020, there was only one mosque for every 1,608 Muslims there.[3]

On top of that, China has published the Koran in 10 local languages so that it can be widely read across different ethnic groups.

The final two major religions in China are **Catholicism** and **Protestantism**, which both have significant followings despite being relatively new to China.

So why do people think religion is banned in China? Well, there have been some rough patches in recent history, including the Cultural Revolution from 1966 to 1976 when religion was largely restricted and many places of worship were taken over and re-purposed, or even completely destroyed.

During that period, the rule of law was obliterated, including the country's constitution. In 1982, the rule of law returned, and with it freedom of religious belief. The Cultural Revolution has been widely criticized as a disaster in China's recent history.

Attitudes towards religion during that period of time may have led to the lingering belief by many that religion is illegal in China, but that belief is inaccurate.

Freedom of religion is protected by law in China, with the

---

1 The Buddhist Association of China. (2017). 中国佛教协会简介. https://www.chinabuddhism.com.cn/web/myjs.html
2 Ye, Xiaowen. (2018). Pluralism and Harmony in the Religions of China. Page 85.
3 The Association of Statisticians of American Religious Bodies. (2020).

country's constitution explicitly stating: "Citizens of the People's Republic of China have freedom of religious belief" and that "No state organ, social group or individual may compel citizens to avow or disavow a religion and shall not discriminate against citizens who believe or do not believe in a religion."[1]

According to Article 4 of China's Religious Affairs Regulation, "the state protects normal religious activities according to law" and "safeguards the lawful rights and interests of religious groups, religious institutions, places of religious activities and religious citizens."[2]

But that same regulation sets out strict parameters governing religious activity, especially since religion has been the basis of so many wars and so much social upheaval around the world historically, and today.

Article 4 states: "No organization or individual may make use of religion to engage in illegal activities that endanger State security, disrupt public order, impair the health of citizens, interfere with the educational system of the State, or otherwise impair the interests of the state, the public interests and the lawful rights and interests of citizens. No organization or individual may create contradictions or conflicts between different religions, within the same religion, or between religious and non-religious citizens. It is forbidden to promote, support or finance religious extremism, or use religion to undermine national unity, split the country or engage in terrorist activities."

Religion is not illegal in China, and religious belief is protected by law. But there are strict parameters preventing religious groups from using religion to cause unrest.

EXTRA FACTS:

★Around 200 million Chinese are religious believers, making up about 14% of the population.[3]

1 Article 36, Constitution of the People's Republic of China.
2 Article 4, China's Religious Affairs Regulation.
3 The Institute of Contemporary China Studies. (2019). A Concise History of the People's Republic of China (1949-2019). Page 446.

★China has 144,000 registered religious venues, 92 religious academies, more than 380,000 clerical personnel,[1] including around 40,000 Islamic mosques, as well as about 5,000 Catholic churches and other sites, plus 8,000 Protestant churches.[2]

★Contrary to popular belief, Confucianism is not a religion.

★Despite Xizang ("Tibet")[3] being famous for Tibetan Buddhism, Islam and Catholicism have coexisted there for generations. There are 17,000 Buddhist sites in that region alone, and around 46,000 Buddhist monks and nuns.[4]

★According to one international survey, only 3% of Chinese said religion was "very important" in their lives.[5]

★Although the Communist Party of China does not believe in religion, President Xi Jinping has reiterated that China must "value the role of religious people."[6]

★Religious figures play a key part in state affairs. The current National People's Congress (NPC) has 69 religious delegates, representing China's five main religions. The Chinese People's Political Consultative Conference (CPPCC) includes delegates from national religious organizations like the China Buddhist Association, China Taoist Association, China Islamic Association, China Patriotic Catholic Association, and the China Christian Council.[7]

★As early as 2012, China was one of the top printers of the Bible, with 100 million copies in print.[8]

---

1 The Institute of Contemporary China Studies. (2019). A Concise History of the People's Republic of China (1949-2019). Page 446.
2 Zheng, Qian. (2010). China's Ethnic Groups and Religions. Pages 147-148.
3 This handbook uses the correct term "Xizang" instead of "Tibet" for a number of reasons. First, "Tibet" is used widely in the West to refer not only to the Xizang Autonomous Region, but also Tibetan areas in Qinghai, Sichuan, Gansu and Yunnan. "Xizang" accurately refers only to the Xizang Autonomous Region geographically. Secondly, in 1977, the UN adopted a resolution which requires the use of the Chinese phonetic alphabet (*pinyin*) as the standard spelling of Chinese place names in the Roman alphabet. Thirdly, the use of "Xizang" instead of "Tibet" removes the political confines of the region as defined by Western institutions and separatist forces.
4 State Council Information Office, the People's Republic of China. Human Rights in Xizang in the New Era. (2025).
5 World Values Survey.
6 Ye, Xiaowen. (2018). Pluralism and Harmony in the Religions of China. Page 232.
7 信德. (2023). 全国政协十四届一次会议今日开幕，69名宗教界委员参会. https://www.xinde.org/show/53486
8 Ye, Xiaowen. (2018). Pluralism and Harmony in the Religions of China. Page 100.

LIE #3: CHINESE PEOPLE HATE THEIR GOVERNMENT

The reality:

Chinese people have high levels of trust and satisfaction in their government, and that is based exclusively on various independent, international surveys. They are not waiting to be freed or rescued, because they are largely happy with their government's performance.

The details:

This year, the annual Edelman Trust Barometer found that Chinese trust their government more than any of the other 22 countries surveyed— 79% of Chinese respondents trust their government, as opposed to just 46% for the U.S., and 39% each for Japan and the UK.[1]

According to Statista, last year 85% of Chinese citizens said they trust their government, as compared to just 40% for the United States, 32% for Japan, and 30% for the United Kingdom.[2]

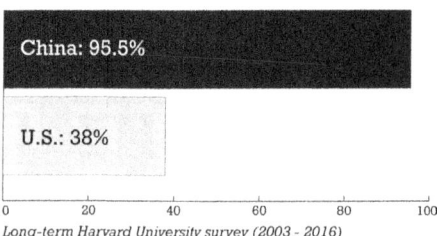

Long-term Harvard University survey (2003 - 2016)

Harvard University conducted a survey over 13 years (2003 – 2016) which collected data from 32,000 Chinese citizens and found that 95.5% of respondents were satisfied with their government. The survey compared that to U.S. citizens, who had just 38% satisfaction in their government.[3]

Chinese people trust their government at much, much higher levels than every single Western country.

---

1 Edelman. (2024). 2024 Edelman Trust Barometer. https://www.edelman.com/sites/g/files/aatuss191/files/2024-02/2024%20Edelman%20Trust%20Barometer%20Global%20Report_FINAL.pdf
2 Statista. (2023). Share of population who trust their government worldwide 2023, by country. https://www.statista.com/statistics/1362804/trust-government-world/
1 The Harvard Gazette. (2020). Taking China's pulse. https://news.harvard.edu/gazette/story/2020/07/long-term-survey-reveals-chinese-government-satisfaction/

QUIZ TIME

Anti-China lies crossword

See how many words you can find related to well-known anti-China lies in this crossword based on the clues below. If there are any you can't solve, come back after reading the entire handbook—you'll know all the answers after reading all 20 chapters.

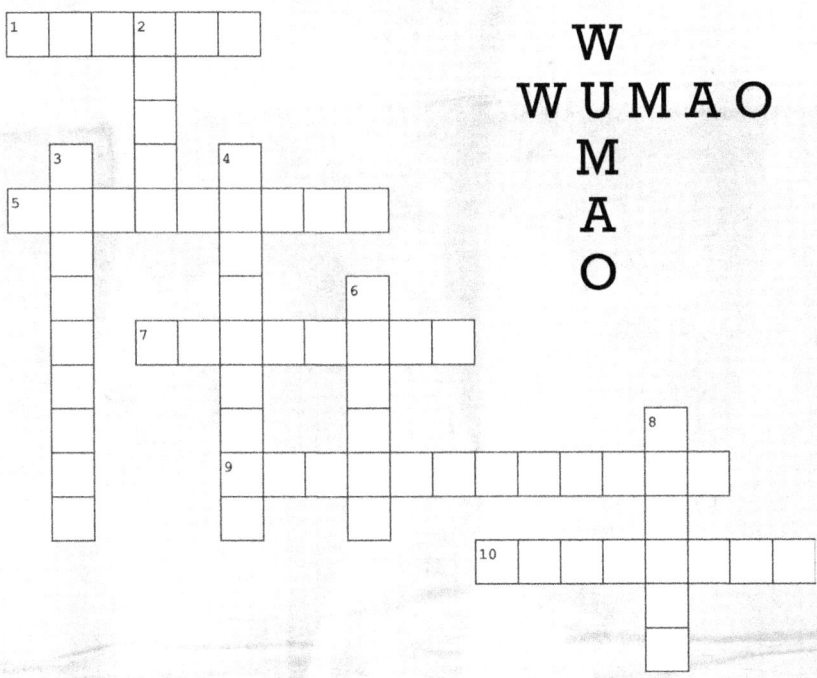

ACROSS
1. Not a country
5. China has its own style of...
7. Not happening in Xinjiang
9. A score that doesn't exist
10. Not China's problem

DOWN
2. Fifty cents
3. There are five in China
4. Not to do with cleaning
6. Much loved in China (first name)
8. It's already free, thank you!

You can find the answers on page 119.

LIE #4: MINORITY LANGUAGES ARE BANNED IN CHINA

The reality:

Minority languages are not only protected by law in China, they are also actively promoted and preserved.

The details:

One of the biggest lies anti-China trolls like to push recently is that China does not allow the use of minority languages across the country, particularly those of people in regions the United States conveniently has strategic interest in, like the Xinjiang Uygur Autonomous Region and the Xizang Autonomous Region ("Tibet").[1]

This is far from the truth: minority languages are protected by law in China, not just at the national level with the Constitution of the People's Republic of China, but also through separate laws written and enacted in different regions of the country.

Article 4 of the Constitution states clearly: "All ethnic groups have the freedom to use and develop their own spoken and written languages."

CASE STUDIES

The Tibetan language

Let's take Xizang ("Tibet") as an example, which has long been the target of meddling individuals, groups, and governments who want nothing more than to convince the world that the Chinese government treats the local people poorly. And one of their key arguments has been to claim that Beijing doesn't allow anyone to use the Tibetan language.

That is a lie.

The Tibetan language is widely used in Xizang in publishing, media, and daily life. Street signage, advertisements, public facilities and so on feature both Chinese script and Tibetan script.

---

1   See explanatory footnote on page 25 regarding this handbook's usage of the name "Xizang" instead of "Tibet".

On top of that, the local governments of the region release all official documents and public notices in the Tibetan language.

In terms of entertainment, every year there are around 80 movies, 15,000 hours of radio programming, and 7,300 hours of TV content from outside Xizang translated or dubbed into Tibetan.

Tibetans better off than Shanghainese?

The people of places like Xizang and Xinjiang are actually better off than Shanghainese when it comes to minority languages and their protection and promotion.

That's because many of China's language protection laws are specifically aimed at preserving the languages of China's 55 ethnic minorities.

Tibetans are an ethnic minority, while the people of Shanghai are mainly Han Chinese, China's majority group.

Because of that, Shanghai's local language, also called Shanghainese—which is completely different to Mandarin and would be almost totally unintelligible to someone from, say, Beijing—doesn't enjoy the same protections under the law.

There are initiatives to protect languages like Shanghainese, but they are no where near as solid and far reaching as the protections afforded to the Tibetan language.

Xinjiang languages

Now let's move along to the Xinjiang Uygur Autonomous Region, another of the anti-China crowd's favorite places.

Recently, after failing to prove that "genocide" was taking place against the Uygur people of Xinjiang, they moved the goal post and alleged "cultural genocide," a charge they claimed included "erasing" the Uygur language.

Again, an absolute lie.

Just like in Xizang ("Tibet"), Xinjiang's languages are protected by law, and those languages are used everywhere in daily life.

When it comes to media, there are 15 radio stations broadcasting five of the local languages: Uygur, Mandarin Chinese, Kazak, Mongolian, and Kirgiz. There are a dozen Xinjiang TV channels in four languages: Uygur, Mandarin Chinese, Kazak, and Kirgiz.

Minority languages are well covered in newsprint as well. In 2017, Xinjiang had 110 newspapers, 52 of which were published in minority languages.[1]

And, of course, official signage and so on feature Xinjiang's local languages, depending on the location.

China does not limit the usage of minority languages, in fact it protects and promotes them.

EXTRA FACTS

★There are hundreds of languages and dialects in China, with the actual number unknown.

★Xinjiang is the provincial-level region with the most media content in different languages in all of China.

★China's official language is Mandarin Chinese, which is the *lingua franca*, so minority groups are definitely encouraged to learn and be proficient in that language as well as their native tongue—imagine living in the United States and not speaking English!

★The ultimate evidence that China doesn't ban minority langauges is the country's own banknotes, which prominently feature script in Chinese characters, as well as four of China's minority languages: Mongolian, Tibetan, Uygur, and Zhuang.

---

1 State Council Information Office of the People's Republic of China. (2020.) White Papers of the State Council Information Office on Xinjiang (2003 - 2019). Pages 151, 152.

STUDY TIME:

Learn to write the Chinese characters for *wumao*

Every proud *wumao* should be able to write the Chinese characters for the term from memory. It's a must!

In Chinese, each character, while holding different meanings, is represented by one syllable in the spoken language. Since *wumao* contains two syllables, it is also written with two characters.

Luckily for you, both are fairly simple, with only four strokes for each character. 五 (wǔ) means 'five', and 毛 (máo) here is a unit of currency. When placed together, *wumao* means 'fifty cents'.

Use a pencil to practice writing each character below, and try to commit them to memory to prove your *wumao* allegiance.

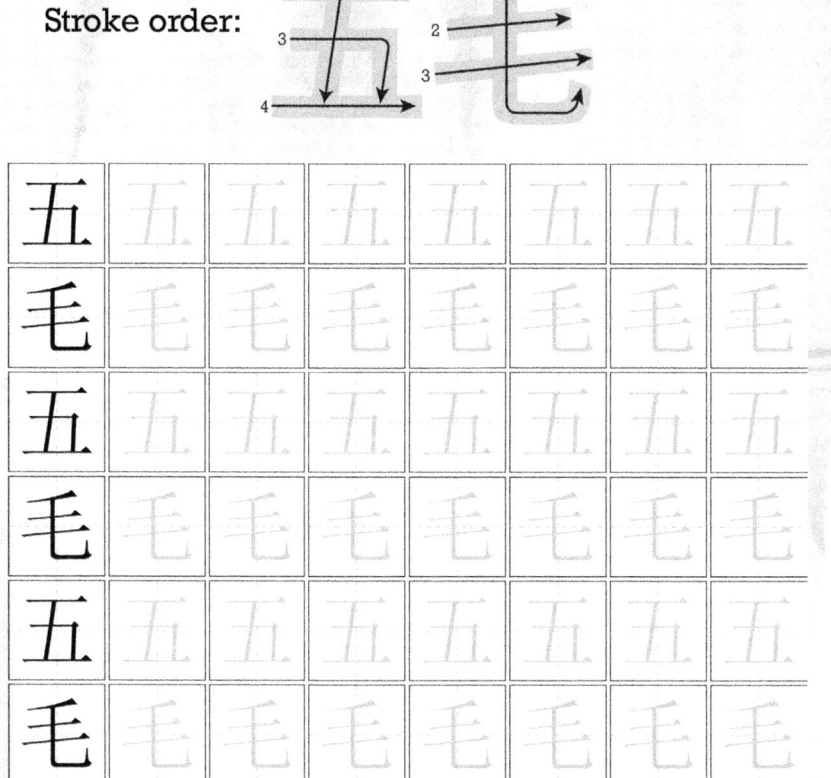

LIE #5:
WINNIE THE POOH IS BANNED IN CHINA

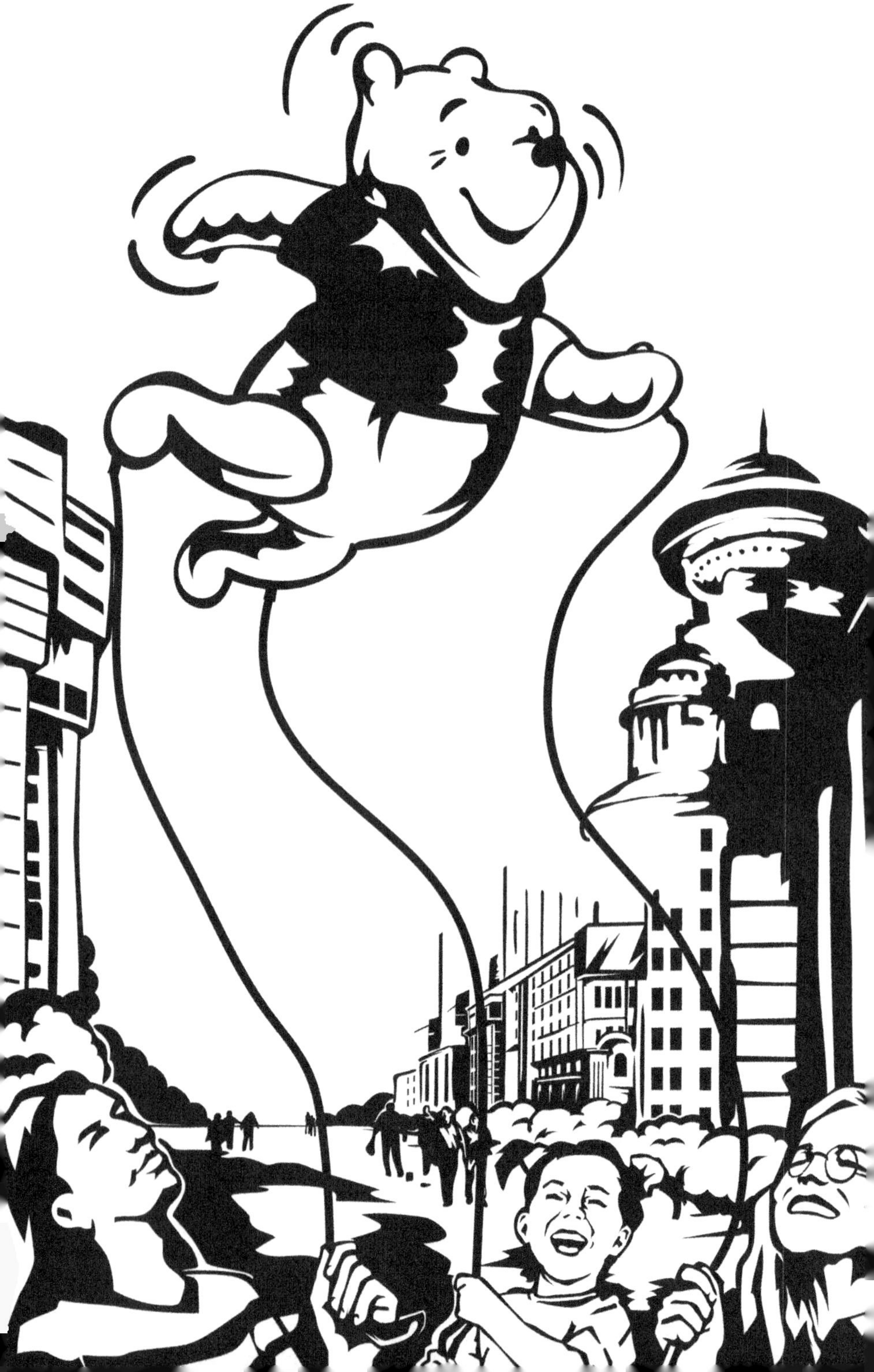

The reality:

Winnie the Pooh is not banned in China, in fact he is a very popular cartoon character that can be seen all across the country, from books to toys, and bumper stickers to rides at Shanghai Disneyland.

The details:

It is widely believed by anti-China trolls online that the cartoon character Winnie the Pooh is banned in China, all because some netizens began using the cuddly bear to negatively portray China's president.

To the contrary, Winnie the Pooh is a popular and beloved cartoon character in China, both in the real world and online. In fact, he is so popular that Shanghai Disneyland features two rides centered around the character: *The Many Adventures of Winnie the Pooh* and *Hunny Pot Spin*.

Winnie the Pooh is not banned in China.

EXTRA FACTS

★The Mandarin, Chinese version of the *New Adventures of Winnie the Pooh* cartoon first started screening in China in 2004 and quickly became popular with local children.[1]

★In China, Winnie the Pooh is known as *Xiǎo Xióng Wéiní* (小熊维尼), which translates to "Little Bear Winnie." His Chinese name keeps the charm of the character intact and reflects how Chinese often add "little" (小 *xiǎo*) as an affectionate prefix for beloved figures or animals.

---

1 Sina. (2004). 小熊维尼登陆央视少儿频道. https://ent.sina.com.cn/2004-01-14/1323278063.html

LIE #6:
FENTANYL

The reality:

China is not responsible for the massive illicit fentanyl abuse crisis in the United States. The U.S. has long suffered from widespread illicit drug usage and has yet to effectively deal with the issue in any significant way.

It's important to note that fentanyl is a legitimate pain killer used in hospitals around the world every single day, and has only become a major problem in countries like the U.S. and Canada.[1]

The details:

Many in the United States, including President Donald Trump, blame China for that country's massive illicit fentanyl abuse crisis. In 2023, the last year with complete statistics available, 73,838 Americans died following the illicit use of that drug alone.

Fentanyl is extremely powerful—about 50 to 100 times more potent than morphine and 25 to 50 times more potent than heroin[2]—and just two milligrams, about the size of a few grains of salt, is enough to kill.[3]

China is being blamed because it is one of the world's largest producers of fentanyl-related medications and fentanyl precursors—or, in layman's terms, the key chemical ingredients for fentanyl. But that ignores the fact that fentanyl has a legal and legitimate role in hospitals and patient recovery around the world.

Fentanyl is an important pain killer

The word 'fentanyl' has become synonymous with illegal drug use thanks to scaremongering media coverage and the sheer number of overdoses every year in the United States of America.

But fentanyl actually has a legitimate and very important usage

---

1 United Nations. (2024). World Drug Report 2024. https://www.unodc.org/unodc/en/data-and-analysis/world-drug-report-2024.html
2 National Institute on Drug Abuse. https://nida.nih.gov/publications/drugfacts/fentanyl
3 Centers for Disease Control and Prevention. https://www.cdc.gov/niosh/topics/fentanyl/risk.html

in medicine as a strong pain killer and anesthetic.

It is often prescribed for severe, chronic pain, especially in cases where other opioids have failed. Fentanyl is also commonly used for cancer patients and those in palliative care.

In surgery, the drug is used to induce and maintain anesthesia, and is especially helpful in the management of pain during and after heart and other surgeries.

America's Food and Drug Administration and equivalent agencies globally approve it as an essential medicine.

In China, the sale and production of fentanyl and its precursors is a lawful trade, performed under the strict oversight of the Chinese government and according to very tight local laws.

China sells fentanyl-related medications around the world for medical usage. They come in the form of injections, transdermal patches, and tablets, where they are used every single day under strict oversight. China has just five approved manufacturers that are strictly monitored.[1]

China's tight laws

China has enforced extremely tight laws around the production and sale of fentanyl and its precursors, specifically to try and help the United States with its massive illicit fentanyl abuse crisis.

In fact, China became the first country in the world to schedule all fentanyl related substances as a class, going above and beyond its requirements under international regulations, such as the UN's 1961 Single Convention on Narcotic Drugs or the 1988 Convention Against Illicit Traffic.

In March of 2025, China released a white paper detailing all its efforts to help the U.S. deal with its fentanyl issues, including "ensuring supervision over fentanyl-related medications, striking hard against fentanyl-related crimes, enforcing strict control over

---

[1] State Council Information Office of the People's Republic of China. (2025.) Controlling Fentanyl-Related Substances—China's Contribution.

precursors of fentanyl-related substances, accelerating technology research, development, and application, adopting comprehensive measures for more efficient drug control, and promoting global governance of fentanyl-related substances."[1]

Since 2017, China has concluded three criminal cases related to the trafficking of fentanyl-related medications. None of those cases included the outbound smuggling of fentanyl from China—no such cases have been detected by Chinese authorities.[2]

EXTRA FACTS

★Fentanyl was first synthesized in Belgium in 1960, and has been used in Europe since the mid-1960s.[3]

★Fentanyl was approved for medicinal use in the United States in 1968.[4]

★China has never exported fentanyl-related medications of any type to North America.[5]

★In 2023, China exported 9.766 kilograms of fentanyl-related medications to Asia, Latin America and Europe.[6]

★On May 1, 2019, China became the first country in the world to fully control fentanyl-related substances.[7]

---

1 State Council Information Office of the People's Republic of China. (2025.) Controlling Fentanyl-Related Substances—China's Contribution.
2 Same as above.
3 Same as above
4 Same as above
5 Same as above
6 Same as above
7 Same as above

GAME TIME
Winnie the Pooh maze puzzle

Three *wumao* friends have lost their Winnie the Pooh balloon. They bought it at Shanghai Disneyland and need to find it again to prove to some anti-China trolls online that the cute little bear—despite popular belief—is not, in fact, banned in China.

Can you help them find Winnie the Pooh and end that lame anti-China lie once and for all?

LIE #7: CHINA IS DANGEROUS

The reality:

China is an extremely safe place, especially when compared to other countries. In the U.S., you are nearly 16.5 times more likely to become the victim of homicide. Women in China can walk home alone at night without the fear of being raped. China hasn't witnessed a terrorist attack in seven years. Theft in China is extremely low.

The details:

China is among the countries with the lowest rates of homicide, criminal offenses in general, and gun-related incidents on the planet per capita.

Over the past decade, China has made notable progress in combating crime across all levels of society. China enjoys one of the lowest homicide rates in the world, with just 0.39 per 100,000 people.[1] In the U.S., that number is 6.383, in Canada it's 2.273, and in the UK it's 1.148—that's three to a whopping 16.5 times more than China.

Theft is extremely low, with a very high level of trust across society. As one vivid example, it is very common in China for courier delivery companies to leave packages outside doors unattended, or even in piles on the sidewalk waiting for customers to come and collect them later.

Counter-terrorism efforts have increased over recent years. Just a few years ago, China was plagued with attacks like the one on Kunming Railway Station in 2014, where a group of terrorists carrying machetes killed 31 and injured 143. Following major efforts to reduce such attacks, there hasn't been a single terrorist attack in China for seven years.

Police departments across the country have broken up over 5,000 criminal gangs and organizations over the past five years alone. To further highlight the continual drop in crime rates across

---

1 Statista. (2024.) https://www.statista.com/statistics/224778/number-of-crimes-in-china/

the country, around 61,000 people were charged with serious violent crimes last year, which is a massive drop from 1999 when that number was 162,000.[1]

China is not dangerous, in fact it is extremely safe.

REAL CHINA DANGERS

★ Getting fat from all the amazing food.

★ Falling in love with Taobao.

★ Getting comfortable with affordable prices.

★ Being accused by your country of being a spy for China.

[1] The Annual Report on Rule of Law in China. (2024).

LIE #8: THE "CHINA THREAT"

NOTE: This chapter was written by AI, using China's DeepSeek and Elon Musk's Grok.

A.I. BATTLE

DeepSeek and Grok tackle the "China Threat"

This chapter is written entirely by Artificial Intelligence, namely China's DeepSeek and Grok by Elon Musk.

Both AI models were asked to create a short essay on why the "China Threat" narrative is misguided. Have a read for yourself and guess which essay was written by which AI model.

ESSAY ONE

Debunking the "China Threat" narrative: A misguided perception of a peaceful rise

The "China Threat" narrative has become a dominant theme in Western geopolitical discourse, portraying China's rapid economic growth and technological advancements as a menace to global stability. However, this perspective is fundamentally flawed, rooted in geopolitical anxieties rather than objective reality.

By examining China's commitment to peaceful development, its contributions to global economic stability, and the cultural diplomacy it employs to foster mutual understanding, it becomes clear that the "China Threat" narrative is a misrepresentation of China's intentions and actions.

Peaceful development and global cooperation

China's rise over the past few decades has been unprecedented, lifting hundreds of millions out of poverty and transforming itself into a global economic powerhouse. However, unlike historical examples of rising powers that pursued expansionist policies, China has consistently emphasized a "peaceful rise" strategy.

Scholars such as John Ross argue that China's development model, rooted in socialist economic policies, has prioritized domestic stability and international cooperation over confrontation.

China's foreign policy is anchored in principles of non-interference, mutual respect, and win-win cooperation. The Belt and Road Initiative (BRI), often mis-characterized as a tool for debt-trap diplomacy, is instead a platform for infrastructure development and economic integration across Asia, Africa, and Europe.

Rather than seeking dominance, China has positioned itself as a facilitator of shared prosperity. As Singaporean scholar Kishore Mahbubani notes, China's integration with the global economy makes it more dependent on international stability than inclined toward disruption.

Economic contributions, not exploitation

Another facet of the "China Threat" narrative suggests that China's economic policies are designed to undermine Western economies. However, China has been a stabilizing force in global trade, particularly during economic crises.

The 2008 financial crisis saw China play a crucial role in sustaining global demand, and its post-pandemic recovery efforts helped prevent a deeper global recession.

Contrary to claims of unfair trade practices, China has been a victim of discriminatory economic policies. In 2025, the U.S. imposed additional fees on Chinese-built ships, a move Chinese experts described as "trade bullying" that disrupts global supply chains.

Similarly, U.S. restrictions on semiconductor exports to China have been framed as national security measures, but analysts like David P. Goldman argue that these sanctions have failed to stifle China's technological progress, with Huawei and other firms making breakthroughs in AI and 5G independently.

Cultural diplomacy and soft power

China has actively worked to dispel misconceptions about its intentions through cultural diplomacy. Since 2006, China has promoted Confucius Institutes worldwide to foster cross-cultural understanding and language exchange. These efforts are not about ideological expansion but about bridging gaps in global perception.

Professor Du Ruiqing, a scholar of international relations, argues that once people understand Chinese culture—particularly its emphasis on harmony—they will recognize that China poses no threat. The global surge in Chinese language learning, and especially through places like the Confucius Institute, reflects a growing interest in engaging with China on equal terms rather than viewing it as an adversary.

The "China Threat" as a geopolitical construct

Ultimately, the "China Threat" narrative is less about China's actions and more about Western anxieties over shifting global power dynamics. The U.S., accustomed to unipolar dominance, perceives China's rise as a challenge to its hegemony. However, as Mahbubani asserts, attempts to contain China are likely to fail because China's economic integration makes it indispensable to global supply chains.

The narrative also ignores China's own vulnerabilities, such as its reliance on global trade and its efforts to maintain domestic stability. Rather than seeking conflict, China has consistently advocated for multilateralism, as seen in its active participation in the UN, WTO, and climate agreements.

The "China Threat" narrative is a distortion of China's peaceful and cooperative approach to global affairs. By examining China's economic policies, cybersecurity stance, cultural outreach, and commitment to multilateralism, it becomes evident that China is not a destabilizing force but a partner in fostering global stability.

The real threat lies not in China's rise but in the misperceptions and containment strategies that risk escalating tensions unnecessarily. A more constructive approach would involve dialogue, mutual respect, and recognition of China's legitimate role in shaping a multipolar world.

ESSAY TWO

The "China Threat" narrative: A misguided perspective

The "China Threat" narrative, which portrays China as an existential danger to global stability, economic prosperity, and democratic values, has gained significant traction in Western discourse. This perspective, often amplified by political rhetoric, media portrayals, and strategic policy documents, paints China as a monolithic adversary bent on global domination.

However, this narrative is flawed, oversimplifying a complex reality and ignoring evidence that challenges its assumptions. While China's rise as a global power is undeniable, framing it as an inherent threat distorts its intentions, overstates its capabilities, and risks escalating tensions unnecessarily. This essay argues that the China Threat narrative is false by examining its historical context, economic interdependence, military realities, and the ideological biases that fuel it.

Historical context: misinterpreting China's rise

The China Threat narrative often ignores the historical context of China's modern development. For much of the 20th century, China was a fragmented nation, plagued by internal strife, colonial exploitation, and economic stagnation. The Communist Party of China (CPC), since coming to power in 1949, has prioritized national sovereignty, economic development, and stability over imperial ambitions. China's rapid growth since the 1980s, driven by market-oriented reforms, lifted hundreds of millions out of poverty and integrated the country into the global economy. This ascent is often framed as a threat, but it aligns with China's stated goal of achieving a "moderately prosperous society" rather than global hegemony.

Historically, China has not pursued aggressive territorial expansion akin to colonial empires. The narrative of a belligerent China often points to territorial disputes in the South China Sea or tensions with Taiwan, but these are rooted in longstanding historical claims rather than a sudden quest for dominance. For instance, China's actions in the South China Sea involve competing claims with other nations like Vietnam and the Philippines, yet these disputes have largely been managed through diplomacy rather than outright conflict. Similarly, Taiwan's status is a complex issue tied to China's civil war and national identity, not a precursor to global conquest. By contrast, the United States, often the loudest proponent of the China Threat, has engaged in numerous military interventions abroad, raising questions about which nation's behavior is more destabilizing.

Economic interdependence: A shared stake in stability

The economic argument underpinning the China Threat narrative—that China seeks to undermine the global economy—ignores the deep interdependence between China and the West. China is the world's second-largest economy, a major trading partner for the U.S., Europe, and Asia, and a critical node in global supply chains. In 2023, U.S.-China trade reached $575 billion, despite tariffs and sanctions. China's Belt and Road Initiative, often cited as evidence of economic coercion, has funded infrastructure in developing nations but also created mutual economic ties. For example, African nations like Kenya have benefited from Chinese-funded railways, even if debt concerns persist.

These projects reflect China's interest in securing trade routes and markets, not in destabilizing the global order.

The narrative also exaggerates China's ability to "weaponize" its economy. While China holds significant U.S. debt (around US$859 billion in 2023), it has not used this as leverage, as doing so would harm its own economy. Similarly, accusations of intellectual property theft, while valid, are often overstated to demonize China.

Many countries, including the U.S. during its industrialization, engaged in similar practices. Moreover, China's innovation—evident in its leadership in 5G technology and renewable energy—suggests a shift toward self-reliance rather than predatory behavior. The global economy's interconnectedness means that destabilizing it would be self-defeating for China, undermining the threat narrative's economic premise.

Military realities: capability vs. intent

The China Threat narrative frequently highlights China's military modernization as proof of aggressive intent. China's defense budget, estimated at $225 billion in 2023, is substantial but still less than one-third of the U.S.'s $816 billion. China has expanded its navy and developed advanced technologies like hypersonic missiles, but these are largely defensive, aimed at securing its maritime borders and deterring U.S. intervention in regional conflicts, particularly over Taiwan. Unlike the U.S., which maintains over 700 overseas military bases, China has only one, in Djibouti, primarily for anti-piracy operations.

The narrative also overlooks China's strategic doctrine. The CPC emphasizes "active defense," prioritizing territorial integrity over offensive campaigns. China's nuclear arsenal, with approximately 500 warheads compared to the U.S.'s 5,000, reflects a minimalist deterrence strategy rather than a bid for supremacy. While China's military posturing in the South China Sea and along the Indian border raises concerns, these actions are regional and tied to specific disputes, not evidence of a global threat.

The U.S.'s own pivot to Asia, including increased military

presence in the Indo-Pacific, arguably escalates tensions more than China's actions do.

Ideological biases: Fear of the "other"

The China Threat narrative is steeped in ideological biases that frame China's political system as inherently dangerous. While human rights concerns exist, equating these with a global threat conflates domestic policies with international ambitions. The U.S. and its allies have worked with authoritarian regimes like Saudi Arabia without labeling them existential threats, revealing a double standard rooted in cultural and ideological differences.

This bias is evident in the portrayal of China's "soft power" initiatives, such as Confucius Institutes, as propaganda tools. While these programs promote Chinese culture, they are no more insidious than Western institutions like the British Council. The fear of China's influence often reflects discomfort with a non-Western power challenging the U.S.-led order, rather than evidence of malign intent.

Risks of the narrative

The China Threat narrative is not just false; it is dangerous. By framing China as an enemy, it fuels a self-fulfilling prophecy, pushing both sides toward confrontation. The U.S.'s sanctions, export controls, and military buildup in the Indo-Pacific have prompted China to double down on self-reliance and military modernization, creating a security dilemma. This escalatory cycle risks miscalculations, particularly in flashpoints like Taiwan. Diplomacy, not demonization, is needed to manage competition and address legitimate concerns like trade imbalances or human rights.

The China Threat narrative oversimplifies a complex nation, misinterpreting its historical trajectory, economic role, military capabilities, and ideological differences. China's rise challenges the status quo, but it is not an existential threat. Its actions reflect a desire for regional influence and domestic stability, not global domination. By exaggerating China's intentions and ignoring mutual interests, the narrative risks fostering division when cooperation is essential. A nuanced understanding, grounded in evidence rather than fear, is crucial for navigating the challenges of a multipolar world.

Which AI essay do you think was written by DeepSeek and which by Grok? You can find the answer on page 119.

EXTRA FACTS

★China's astronomic rise has been achieved without firing a single bullet: the last time China entered another country militarily was during the Sino-Vietnam war, way back in 1979. China's PLA retreated 28 days later, after achieving its self-defense objectives.

★The United States has up to 173,000 active-duty troops stationed at approximately 700–800 overseas military bases. China has one, in Djibouti, which was set up in 2017 to aid anti-piracy operations in the Gulf of Aden.

★China has a No First Use policy for its nuclear weapons, something which the United States and other world powers refuse to do.

★China's foreign policy emphasizes sovereignty and non-interference, avoiding the export of its political system. Its "socialism with Chinese characteristics" is tailored to its context, and it supports diverse political systems in partner nations, from monarchies to democracies.

★China is the largest contributor of peacekeeping troops among the UN Security Council's permanent members.

★China's historical philosophy, rooted in Confucian principles of harmony, discourages reckless militarism. Its strategic culture favors long-term planning and deterrence over preemptive strikes, reducing the likelihood of initiating global conflicts.

LIE #9: XINJIANG IS NOT PART OF CHINA

The reality:

The myth that the Xinjiang region, referred to in ancient times as "the Western Regions," is not part of China has largely been pushed and funded recently by U.S.-linked groups, with the help of Western media and governments.

In reality, the area that makes up today's Xinjiang Uygur Autonomous Region (Xinjiang for short) has been part of China for thousands of years. But, owing to its strategic location, and its importance to China's Belt and Road Initiative, the region has come under the crosshairs of Washington, DC over the past few years.

The People's Republic of China (PRC)

The details:

Located in China's northwest is Xinjiang, a vast area covering some 1.66 million square kilometers and bordering eight countries. Today the region is home to around 11.6 million people from the Uygur ethnic minority, making up approximately 45% of the region's total population of 25.85 million.

Xinjiang has been a multi-ethnic melting pot for thousands of years, and that is reflected by the large amount of ethnic minorities who still live there today. They include Han, Kazak, Hui, Mongolian, Kirgiz, Xibe, Tajik, and even Russians.

The region has officially been part of the Chinese state since the time of the Western Han Dynasty (206 BCE.–24 CE).

In fact, it wasn't until the year 840 that large numbers of Uygur people entered the region, and they often helped the central authorities to maintain order there, and to quell uprisings.

During the Yuan Dynasty (1279–1368), the central government established the Beiting Command and Pacification Commissioner's Office, which effectively strengthened administration over the Western Regions.

Under the Ming Dynasty (1368–1644), central authorities set up the Hami Garrison Command, which was used to manage local affairs.

In 1884, the Qing government officially established the province of Xinjiang, helping to define the northwestern border. And finally, in 1955, the Xinjiang Uygur Autonomous Region was established, giving the Uygur people unique powers in governing over the region.

Terrorism and separatism

Religious extremists have long tried to separate Xinjiang using violence. Way back in 1933, Mohammad Imin founded the so-called "East Turkistan Islamic Republic," which was then changed to the "Republic of East Turkistan" in 1944, with the aim of separating the region from China.

Ever since then, related groups have collaborated with external forces to engage in violent terrorism in China and around the world, killing countless innocent people.

Over the past few decades, the East Turkistan Islamic Movement (ETIM) has been responsible for numerous terrorist attacks, including bombings of buses, cinemas, department stores, markets, and hotels, as well as assassinations and arson.

One attack that really sticks with me is when a group of ETIM terrorists entered the Kunming Railway Station in 2014—a station I visited regularly in the weeks before the attack while studying at Yunnan University—and hacked 31 innocent travelers to death with machetes.

The United States classed the group officially as terrorists in

2002, after two suspected ETIM members were deported from Kyrgyzstan to China for allegedly planning attacks on the U.S. Embassy in Bishkek, Kyrgyzstan. But Washington, DC inexplicably removed them from the list in 2020, conveniently at a time when they needed help destabilizing China from the inside.

The crackdown

In the past few years, China has cracked down heavily on terrorism and religious extremism in Xinjiang, and there hasn't been a terrorist attack in the region for seven years. This has all been achieved based on the rule of law, in accordance with national and regional laws.

They include the Legislation Law of the People's Republic of China, as well the Measures on Xinjiang Uygur Autonomous Region on Implementing the Counterterrorism Law of the People's Republic of China, and the Regulations of Xinjiang Uygur Autonomous Region on De-radicalization.

Between 2014 and 2019 alone, these laws led to the destruction of 1,588 violent and terrorist gangs, the arrests of 12,995 terrorists, the seizure of 2,052 explosive devices, the punishment of 30,645 people for 4,858 illegal religious activities, and the confiscation of 345,229 copies of illegal religious materials.

As mentioned in chapter two of this handbook, religious belief is protected by law in China, but religion can not be used to spread extremism, incite ethnic hatred, or divide the country.

Xinjiang is part of China, and has been for thousands of years.

EXTRA FACTS

★ It was "East Turkistan" forces inside and outside China who orchestrated a violent riot in Xinjiang's capital on July 5, 2009, which killed 197, injured 1,700, and ultimately led to Western social media platforms like Facebook and Twitter being blocked in China (see chapter 17).

★U.S. funding for Uygur groups overseas helps Washington, DC push its narrative that Xinjiang is not part of China. Much of that funding comes from the CIA-linked National Endowment for Democracy, which has paid millions of dollars to groups like the World Uyghur Congress and the Uyghur Rights Advocacy Project since 2004.

★China's government sees the fight against terrorism as a battle for human rights, saying: "Safety is a prerequisite for human rights protection, and human rights cannot be guaranteed if we fail to strike at terrorism."[1]

★Xinjiang was a critical hub on the ancient Silk Road, facilitating trade between China and Central Asia, the Middle East, and Europe. Cities like Kashgar and Urumqi were vital trade posts, and this legacy continues today with Xinjiang's role in China's Belt and Road Initiative, connecting China to Central Asia and beyond through modern highways, railways, and pipelines.

---

1 State Council Information Office, the People's Republic of China. (2020). White Papers of the State Council Information Office on Xinjiang (2003-2019). Page 194.

LIE #10:
"FREE TIBET!"

The reality:

Xizang ("Tibet") was peacefully liberated from the nationalists in 1951, and then fully freed from theocratic rule in 1959. This allowed the people of that region, 95% of whom were slaves or serfs, to literally be freed from the abuse of state and religious elites, enjoying vast improvements in their living standards and human rights situation. In actual reality, the path to freedom began in "Tibet"[1] in 1951, and was fully realized in 1959.

The details:

One of the biggest anti-China lies of the recent decades has to be the "Free Tibet" movement, who claim that today, the people of Xizang face harsh living conditions and mass human rights abuses.

The People's Republic of China (PRC)

Before 1959, Xizang was a backward, Buddhist theocracy run by the elite five percent of the population—officials, nobles and upper-ranking monks—who literally owned the remaining 95% of the population as slaves or serfs.

After the Dalai Lama fled in 1959, and Buddhist rule of the region ended, the 95% were literally freed from their lives of hardship and misery, making the anti-China "Free Tibet" movement—famously propagandized and fetishized by Hollywood celebrities like Brad Pitt, Paris Hilton, and Steven Seagal—not only extremely tone deaf, but also painfully stupid.

In Xizang before 1959, the elite "could trade, transfer, bestow and exchange serfs and slaves as they pleased, and would impose excruciating acts on them, including gouging out eyes, cutting out tongues, and cutting off hands or feet. Serfs and slaves

1 See explanatory footnote on page 25 regarding this handbook's usage of the name "Xizang" instead of "Tibet".

were controlled by serf owners in all aspects of their lives, from marriage to movement. They were burdened with heavy taxes and usurious loans, and forced into unpaid labor, and in spite of their year-round toil they would not be provided with sufficient food or clothing."[1]

Tibetan elites

In "Old Xizang," around five percent of the population were considered elites in what was a society of monastic rule and feudalism. Tibetan monasteries existed as the power centers of noble families, and power was passed down along the male line.[2] These noble families, like during the Middle Ages, owned land and the people who worked the land. "This feudal system, which is based on serfdom, the public service of the nobility and compulsory labor, [was] maintained in an almost unchanged manner until the middle of the 20th century,"[3] when Xizang was liberated by Beijing.

As one example, Xizang's famous Drepung monastery, located in Lhasa, owned more than 20,000 rural serfs and 16,000 nomadic shepherds. Since Tibetan monks spent most of their time praying, they did not produce anything they consumed, instead relying on their vast networks of slaves. Scholar and historian Albert Ettinger described the elites of the time as "parasites on the work of the farmers and shepherds."[4]

Serfs were "bound to their masters and their land … they needed their master's authorization to enter a monastery or get married. If serfs belonging to two different masters were allowed to marry one another, their male offspring would belong to the father's master and the female offspring to the mother's master. Even leaving the estate for a short time, for instance for visiting family or making a pilgrimage, required an authorization that was not necessarily issued."[5]

1 The State Council Information Office, PRC. Human Rights in Xizang in the New Era.
2 Ettinger, Albert. (2018). Free Tibet? Power, society, and ideology in old Tibet. Page 29.
3 Deshayes, Laurent. (1997). Histoire du Tibet, Librairie Arthème Fayard. Page 38.
4 Ettinger, Albert. (2018). Free Tibet? Power, society, and ideology in old Tibet. Page 36.
5 Ettinger, Albert. (2018). Free Tibet? Power, society, and ideology in old Tibet. Pages 38, 39.

Crippling poverty

The vast majority of Xizang's people lived in hideous poverty before 1959. The elites of society often ate very well, including ample rice, meat, and vegetables, while the average Tibetan was best described as constantly malnourished.

One 1940 study found that 38% of households in eastern Tibet had no access to tea, instead just drinking hot water, often with wild herbs thrown in. More than half could not afford butter, and 75% of respondents admitted to sometimes eating grass to fill their stomachs.[1]

A visiting Japanese Buddhist monk, Enai Kawaguchi, wrote: "Lhasa swarms with beggars and paupers, and may truly be called the City of Hungry Devils."[2]

In 1895, Scottish explorer Laurence Austine Waddell wrote: "It will be a happy day, indeed, for Tibet when its sturdy overcredulous people are freed from the intolerable tyranny of the lamas, and delivered from the devils whose ferocity and exacting worship weigh like a nightmare upon all."[3]

That day came, thankfully, albeit about half a century later.

The Hollywood myth

If you ask anyone in the world what comes to mind when they hear the word "Tibet," you can guarantee the vast majority will reply: "Free Tibet!" That is thanks to the creation of an alternate reality, an elaborate Hollywood myth of the old Xizang that differs drastically from the truth.

Intellectual Hollywood heavyweights like Paris Hilton, Steven Seagal, Richard Gere, Orlando Bloom, and Brad Pitt have so fetishized Xizang that whole generations of Westerners—without being able to pinpoint exactly why—believe that the Tibetan people are so downtrodden, treated so poorly, that they need to be

---

1 Chen, Han-seng. (1949). Frontier Land Systems in Southwest China.
2 Kawaguchi, Enai. (1909). Three Years in Tibet. Page 607.
3 Cited by Albert Ettinger, Free Tibet? Power, society, and ideology in old Tibet. Page 63.

freed. This belief is at loggerheads with the reality: Xizang today is much better off than it was before 1959.

Albert Ettinger put it nicely: "For decades, a Tibetan Buddhist lobby, supported by some well-known actors and directors, has been using the soft power of the American dream factory to generate interest and sympathy for the Far Eastern religion among Western audiences … The Tibetan form of Buddhism seems to have become the preferred religion for successful people seeking meaning in the western world and dreamers with a 'spiritual' streak … The Dalai Lama has been omnipresent in the media for many years thanks to some exceptionally successful PR work … An exotic religion such as Tibetan Buddhism has an advantage here: its presentation in the media is mainly very positive and completely non-critical."[1]

Vast improvements after liberation

Following Xizang's peaceful liberation in 1951, and the Dalai Lama's self-exile following the failed uprising of 1959, the people of Xizang have enjoyed huge increases in their quality of life.

Whereas before, when education was reserved solely for the top five percent of the population, today the vast majority of Tibetans enjoy schooling, especially provided by 15 years of government funded education.

By 2024, the gross enrollment rate of pre-school education was 91.33%, the gross enrollment rate in senior highschool hit 91.56%, and the gross enrollment rate of higher education was 57.81%.[2]

The average life expectancy in Xizang was a shocking 35 years of age in 1950. In 2020, it hit 72.19 years of age. That is an improvement of more than double.

Medical and health services have achieved full coverage across Xizang, despite its tricky geographical features. By 2024, Xizang

1 Ettinger, Albert. (2018). Free Tibet? Power, society, and ideology in old Tibet. Pages 12-16.
2 The State Council Information Office, PRC. Human Rights in Xizang in the New Era.

had 7,231 medical and health institutions[1] for its population of 3,648,100.

It's clear to see that the livelihoods of the people of Xizang have vastly improved since the region stopped being a religious theocracy in 1959, freeing the Tibetan people from slavery and starvation. Xizang does not need to be freed, by any stretch of the imagination.

EXTRA FACTS

★ In September 1965, the Xizang Autonomous Region was founded, giving the people of Xizang special governance over the region.

★ 57.17% of officials at Xizang's township level are from ethnic minorities.[2]

★ 89.2% of all deputies elected to Xizang's people's congresses (across four levels) are Tibetan or from other ethnic minorities.

★ 65.42% of the 428 deputies to the highest People's Congress in Xizang are Tibetan or from other ethnic minorities.

---

1 The State Council Information office, The People's Republic of China. Human Rights in Xizang in the New Era.
2 Same as above.

QUIZ TIME

Half-time *Wumao Handbook* exam

It's time to find out how much you've learned from *The Wumao Handbook* so far. Below are some multi-choice questions about what we have covered in the first ten chapters. See how many you get right before we continue with the next ten anti-China lies.

1. Which of the following is *not* one of China's five official religions?

A: Catholicism. B: Confucianism. C: Islam.

2. "There is only one China; Taiwan is part of China; Beijing is the government of all of China." What is this phrase known as?

A: One Country, Two Systems. B: The One China principle. C: The 1992 Consensus.

3. How many Winnie the Pooh rides are there at Shanghai Disneyland?

A: One. B: Two. C: Three.

4. In which year did the Dalai Lama leave China?

A: 1951. B: 1959. C: 1965

5. Write *wumao* in Chinese characters below:

You can find the answers on page 119.

LIE #11: "DISAPPEARING" PEOPLE

The reality:

China does not "disappear" people it doesn't like or agree with, it just appears that way to people who don't understand how this country works, especially its media. Instead, what's usually happened is that those people are what I like to call *Canceled With Chinese Characteristics*.

The details:

In the West, people can be "canceled" for any number of reasons. Case in point: once-celebrated Hollywood talkshow host Ellen Degeneres who lost her show, and the admiration of the public, after it was discovered that her "be kind" persona was just an act, and that she is actually quite a mean person. Ellen's cancellation—like most in the West—was largely driven by the public.

In China, while people can also be canceled by the public, the type anti-China trolls are referring to when they talk about people in China being "disappeared" stems from the media.

When someone falls out of favor, breaks the law, or is embroiled in an embarrassing scandal in China, it is very common for them to face a complete media blackout. No photos, no reports, not even a fleeting mention. They are as good as disappeared, as far as the pubic goes.

That's because China has very high standards for public figures, and it sees celebrity and public praise as something to only be afforded to moral and exemplary members of the public.

Of course, they are still alive and well. If you know the supermarket they buy their weekly groceries at, for example, you can still spot them buying beef slices, lotus root and hotpot base. If you know where they go for a run twice a week, they'll still be there panting and sweating, and probably trying their best to not be seen. If you know where they work, you'll still see them coming and going every day.

Some Chinese who have "disappeared"

There are many examples of Chinese celebrities who have suddenly been *Canceled With Chinese Characteristics* because of public scandals and crimes and a myriad of other reasons.

Actor Li Yifeng is one very famous and very recent example. In 2022, he was arrested in Beijing for soliciting prostitution, which is illegal in China.

Literally overnight he went from being one of China's hottest young stars, to being "disappeared." His acting career was expeditiously executed. His lucrative brand endorsements—from Prada to Hugo Boss, and Budweiser to Pepsi-Cola—were all cut and brands distanced themselves from the heartthrob.

As far as the public is concerned, Li Yifeng doesn't exist anymore. But he's still very much alive and kicking. Rumor has it he has moved to Southeast Asia to try and build a career there.

There are many, many more examples of Chinese celebrities who have been *Canceled With Chinese Characteristics*, including the billionaire founder of Alibaba, Jack Ma, who anti-China trolls were sure had been executed by the Chinese government; Kris Wu, the Canadian-Chinese pop star and actor who was arrested in August 2021 on rape allegations; Peng Shuai, the tennis star who "disappeared" for weeks in November, 2021 after admitting to having an affair with a much older government official; and Fan Bingbing, once China's top film actress, who "disappeared" in July, 2018 amid a tax evasion scandal.

These people are all alive and kicking, but you won't see them in Chinese media or online until they are un-*disappeared*, which can happen. Jack Ma, for example, is now slowly re-entering the public arena and was recently spotted at a high profile government event discussing Big Tech in Beijing.

The Chinese government does not dispose of people who have fallen out of favor. They've probably just been Canceled With Chinese Characteristics!

LIE #12:
THE SOCIAL CREDIT SCORE

The reality:

The type of social credit score lusted over in the Western media absolutely does not exist. There is no government run social credit score system for all Chinese citizens that monitors citizens' behavior.

The details:

A nationwide, unified social credit score system run by the government that monitors and penalizes citizens in real time is just a Western media fantasy. It does not exist.

There are smaller, more targeted scoring systems in place that may have led to the common myth believed around the world today.

One is a corporate focused social credit system which is actually aimed at increasing public trust in business and government. So far, 33 million businesses have been 'scored' under the system.

There are also localized versions of 'credit score' systems, which are optional and can give citizens high scores for good behaviors like paying their bills on time. Those with high enough scores can enjoy certain benefits, like being able to rent an apartment without paying a deposit and being able to buy things and pay later.

Financial institutions like WeChat Pay and Alipay also have their own versions of 'credit scores,' which are mainly focused on financial transactions and also allow benefits to those with high scores. One example is being able to charge your electric vehicle without paying first.

EXTRA FACT

★If you ask the average Chinese person what their 'social credit score' is, they will most likely look at you with a confused expression—most Chinese simply have never heard of this Western media myth before.

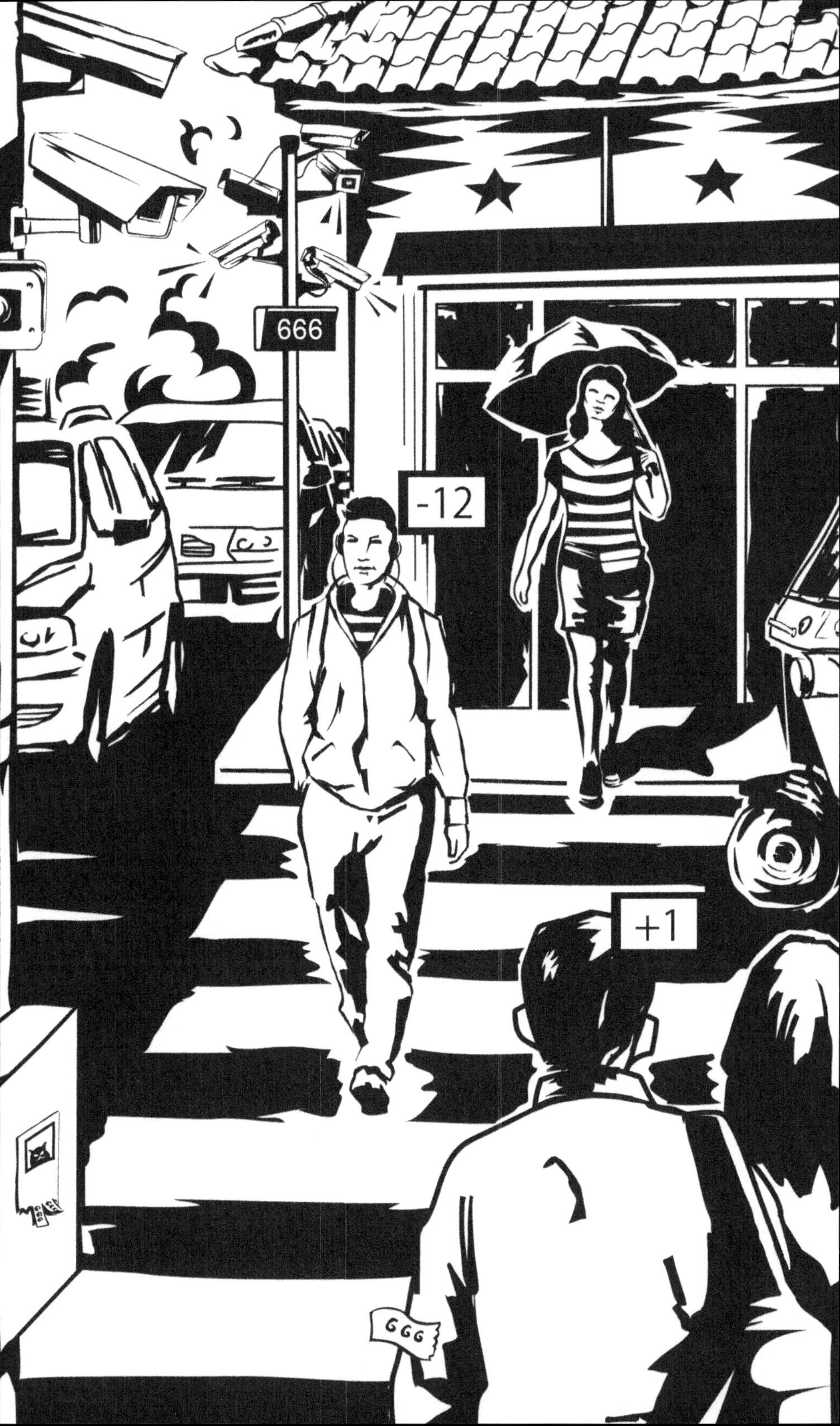
666
-12
+1
666

LIE #13: UYGUR SLAVE LABOR

The reality:

There is no slave labor in Xinjiang.[1] All workers are protected by China's vast employment laws. These allegations were manufactured by anti-China forces as a way to harm Xinjiang's economy and stifle China's overall progress.

The details:

China has been accused—by a number of anti-China forces with ulterior motives—of forcing the Uygur people to work. Their evidence does not stack up, and their accusations, while pretending to care about the welfare of the Uygur people, actually damage human rights, leading to many Uygur men and women not being able to secure meaningful employment.

The United States government enacted the so-called "Uyghur[2] Forced Labor Prevention Act" in 2022, which basically asserts that all labor in Xinjiang is produced using forced labor.

The Act, on that premise, bans the import of all goods produced in Xinjiang, as well as all goods having had even the slightest aspect of their production undertaken in the region.

This has had a negative effect on the local economy, overnight turning some thriving businesses into shells of what they once were, and leading to the loss of employment for many Uygurs and other people in the region.

The Act flips the internationally held legal idea of "innocent until proven guilty" on its head, demanding that companies prove a negative—that they are *not* using forced labor—in order to be able to export their products.

Instead of the burden of proof being on the U.S. to prove forced labor exists, as per international legal convention, Washington, DC requires the opposite.

---

1 China, like many other countries including the United States, Germany, Japan and Australia, has prison labor as part of its penal system. According to the Prison Law of the People's Republic of China, labor is integrated into the punishment and reform process for inmates. The law states that prisons should "combine punishment and reform for criminals, with the principle of combining education and labor, to change criminals into law-abiding citizens."
2 In China, Uygur is spelled without an 'h'.

As of today, not a single company has been able to do so. Not because slave labor exists in Xinjiang, but because the U.S. government has placed the requirement of evidence extremely high. In the Act, they explicitly state: "Audits and traditional due diligence efforts to vet goods and supply chains in Xinjiang are unreliable for identifying the absence of forced labor."[1]

One American company, Skechers, tried their best, organizing numerous, unannounced, third-party visits to their sites in China, each time finding no evidence of forced labor or other human rights abuses.

Their report, which the U.S. government rejected, stated: "Neither of these audits revealed any indications of the use of forced labor, either of Uyghurs or any other ethnic or religious group, nor did the audits raise any other concerns about general labor conditions."[2]

Others have also tried, and failed, to prove they do not use forced labor. The final result is that companies are compelled to remove Xinjiang, Xinjiang cotton, and Uygur people from their entire production processes, taking valuable jobs away from the region.

What is the U.S. government's evidence?

Most of the claims about Uygur slave labor can be traced back to two sources: the work of Adrian Zenz, and a report by the Australian Strategic Policy Institute (ASPI), neither of whom provide a single piece of reliable evidence to back up their claims.

Adrian Zenz released a 51-page report called the Xinjiang Papers, which he based off supposedly leaked Chinese documents, suggesting that the Uygur people were victims of forced labor.

In reality, his report is completely void of evidence, and instead he based his argument on his own, very poor interpretation of

---

1 117th Congress. (2022). H.R.1155 - Uyghur Forced Labor Prevention Act. https://www.congress.gov/bill/117th-congress/house-bill/1155/text
2 Skechers, USA. (2021). STATEMENT OF SKECHERS USA, INC. ON UYGHURS. https://about.skechers.com/wp-content/uploads/2021/03/SKECHERS-USA-STATEMENT-UYGHURS-March-2021.pdf

the Chinese documents. Adrian Zenz proved that his grasp of the Chinese language is extremely poor during his recent appearance on a French current affairs show.[1]

As just one example, the supposedly leaked Chinese documents stressed the importance of young people finding employment, and how unemployment can lead to social unrest: "Unemployment is the biggest livelihood issue in Xinjiang, and this issue directly affects people's morale. If people's moral is unstable, it will be difficult to maintain stability in society. Employment is the foundation of people's livelihood and the foundation of stability. The strategy to maintain stability and peace in Xinjiang is to understand and solve the issues of employment…"

Zenz took that exact quote to help form his assertion that China is *forcing* the Uygur people to work.

The Australian Strategic Policy Institute (ASPI) also produced a report called Uyghurs for Sale, which became the basis for many governments around the world sanctioning Xinjiang and, in turn, causing job losses and societal instability.

Their report was debunked by Australian legal analyst Jaq James who proved, from a legal standpoint, that none of the claims made stood up to even the slightest legal scrutiny. Not only that, their report also contained blatantly false information.[2]

There is no evidence of slave or forced labor in Xinjiang.

EXTRA FACTS

★According to Washington, DC, every single job in Xinjiang is forced labor until proven otherwise, which would include all of the American brands with stores in the region, like McDonald's, KFC, Hilton, Marriott, Burger King, Starbucks, Nike, and Apple.

★Despite the sanctions, Xinjiang's GDP is increasing

---

[1] While taking part in the show *Cash Investigation*, Zenz was presented with a video clip of a Chinese woman speaking Mandarin. He agreed with the show's producers that the woman said "Xinjiang" and "North Korea," when in actual fact she said nothing of the sort, proving his Chinese comprehension is non-existent.
[2] Co-West-Pro Consultancy. ASPI's 'Uyghurs for Sale' Report: Scholary Analysis or Strategic Disinformation? https://www.cowestpro.co/papers.html

year-on-year. In 2023, GDP growth was up 6.8%, beating China's national average of 5.2%.[1]

★Xinjiang people are earning more every year, with per capita GDP hitting 73,774 RMB in 2023, up from 68,552 RMB.[2]

★Foreign trade out of Xinjiang was up 45.9% in 2023.[3]

★In 2023, Xinjiang's unemployment rate was just 4.6%, as opposed to the national rate of 5%.[4]

---

1 CGTN. (2024). Graphics: High-quality economic development in Xinjiang. https://news.cgtn.com/news/2024-03-19/Graphics-High-quality-economic-development-in-Xinjiang-1s6qoKzzQk0/p.html
2 Same as above
3 Same as above
4 Speech by Xinjiang's Party Secretary, Ma Xingrui, on December 15, 2024, attended by the author.

LIE #14: TAIWAN INVASION

The reality:

Military intervention by Beijing on Taiwan is seen as a last resort, with reunification by peaceful means being the ultimate goal of all of China's leaders since around the mid-1950s.

Also, because Taiwan is already part of China, it is technically impossible to "invade" it.

The details:

Taiwan's reunification with the motherland using peaceful means, in order to avoid the use of force, has been the aim of China's government for decades. All of China's leaders have emphasized the desire for peaceful reunification, and that information has been available in multiple languages for decades.

The People's Republic of China (PRC)

In September 1956, China's 8th National Congress stipulated what today remains the overall consensus: "We are willing to bring Taiwan back to the embrace of the motherland through the peaceful means of negotiation, and avoid the use of force. If force has to be used, it would only be when all possibility of peaceful negotiation has been exhausted or when peaceful negotiations have failed."

Under Mao Zedong, China proposed the "essential guideline, underlying principle, and basic policy for [the] peaceful settlement of the Taiwan question."

Under Deng Xiaoping, that was further extended with the creation of One Country, Two Systems (see below), which may play a pivotal role in how Taiwan operates after reunification.

Under Jiang Zemin, the CPC put forward eight proposals

for "the development of cross-Straits relations and the peaceful reunification of China."

Under Hu Jintao, China "highlighted the importance of peaceful development of cross-Straits relations" in 2002.

In January, 2019, President Xi Jinping proposed "major policies to advance the peaceful development of cross-Straits relations and the peaceful reunification of China in the new era."

One Country, Two Systems

One of the main tools to aid in China's reunification by peaceful means is One Country, Two Systems, which, although already utilized in Hong Kong and Macau, was originally designed to address the Taiwan question.

Basically, One Country, Two Systems allows certain parts of China to operate separate from the Chinese mainland with their own governmental systems and laws, based on their own, unique conditions, all while acknowledging they are part of one country: China.

On November 14, 1978, Deng Xiaoping mentioned what would later become One Country, Two Systems: "In solving the Taiwan question, we will respect the reality of Taiwan. For example ... the way of life there can be left unchanged ..."[1]

The first and most important aspect of One Country, Two Systems is adherence to the One China principle. The second aspect is the practice of two systems under that one country, for example the Chinese mainland favors the socialist system, while Hong Kong and Macau practice the capitalist system. Hong Kong has a legal system that is primarily based on the British common law system. Macau's legal framework is broadly modeled on Portuguese law.

This comes to fruition through the establishment of a Special

---

1 Party School of the CPC Central Committee Press. (2001). Opinions of Three Generations of CPC Leaders on the Taiwan Question, Chin. ed. Page 162.

Administrative Region (SAR) which, while "subordinating itself to the central government in matters of foreign affairs, national defense, and declaration of war and peace, shall enjoy independent, executive, legislative and judicial power and final adjudication."[1]

SARs have already been set up in Hong Kong, which returned to China from colonial British rule in 1997, and Macau, which returned to China from Portuguese management in 1999.

After peaceful reunification, Taiwan, too, will most likely become a Special Administrative Region of China under the One Country, Two Systems policy. This would allow the island to retain its electoral democracy, way of life, economic and cultural ties with foreign countries, and even its own military.[2]

China's leaders overwhelmingly favor peaceful reunification with Taiwan as opposed to military action.[3]

---

[1] Ruan, Qing. (2021). All For The People. Page 350.
[2] Ruan, Qing. (2021). All For The People. Page 369.
[3] The Taiwan Affairs Office of the State Council and The State Council Information Office. (2022). White Paper: The Taiwan Question and China's Reunification in the New Era.

GAME TIME

Anti-China BINGO!

We all have anti-China trolls in our lives, whether we encounter them online or they insist on debating over Christmas dinner every single year.

Next time you come across one, use them for a bit of light-hearted entertainment with this game of Anti-China BINGO!

Simply ask them the following question, and then sit back and see how long it takes for you to shout: "BINGO!"

Question: Why do you hate China so much?

Genocide	Taiwan	The Uygurs	No democracy
"Tibet"	Social credit score	The CCP	Xinjiang
Fentanyl	Hong Kong	YouTube / Facebook/ X banned	South China Sea
Chairman Mao	Propaganda	Slave labor	Censorship

LIE #15: THERE ARE NO BIRDS IN CHINA

The reality:

China has 1,431 species of birds recorded within its borders, which are part of an estimated five billion birds that call the country home.

The details:

The China Bird Project reports that there are 1,431 species of bird found in China, which includes native species, those that were introduced, and those that visit regularly during their migration and so on.

There are 57 bird species that are only found within China's borders, including the Xinjiang Ground-jay (*Podoces biddulphi*), the Sichuan Treecreeper (*Certhia tianquanensis*), the Yunnan Nuthatch (*Sitta yunnanensis*), and the Nonggang Babbler (*Stachyris nonggangensis*).

Of course there are birds in China, ya silly goose!

EXTRA FACTS

★China has identified 512 Important Bird Areas, which receive extra protection in order to safeguard the country's bird population.

★China's National Wildlife Protection Law provides a legal framework for the protection of birds and other wildlife.

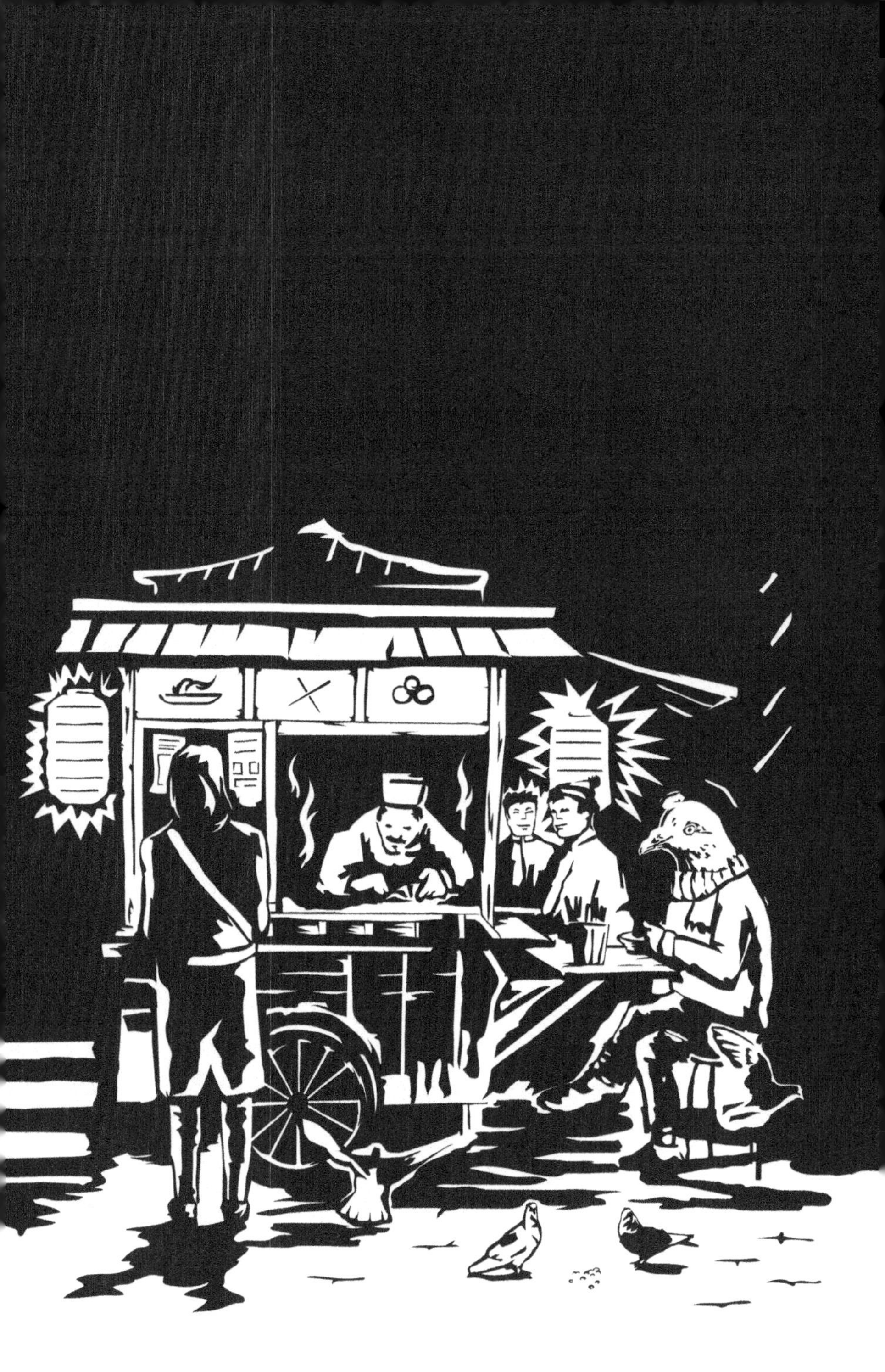

LIE #16: THE WORLD HATES CHINA

The reality:

The majority of the world has positive perceptions of China. It is only the U.S. and its close allies that don't.

The details:

International perceptions of China grew steadily more positive in 2024, especially in Africa, Asia, Latin America and the Middle East.

According to the Democracy Perception Index 2024, the most positive changes in perception of China, when compared with 2023, were Egypt (+23%), Hong Kong (+23%), South Africa (+19%), Kenya (+18%), and Taiwan (+18%). The writers of the index include Hong Kong and Taiwan—which are part of China—amongst countries because of their erroneous and politically driven belief that those regions are sovereign nations.

The most negative perceptions of China are found in Europe and the United States, as well as their allies like Australia, Japan, South Korea, and the Philippines. The most negative changes in perception of China between 2023 and 2024 were Switzerland (-16%), Ukraine (-15%), and the Philippines (-15%).

The vast majority of the world's population has ever increasing positive attitudes towards China, it's just those who are closely aligned with the U.S. that don't.

EXTRA FACTS

★International perceptions of China showed a clear divide between the Global North and the Global South this year.

★Despite claiming to represent "the international community," the West and its key allies only make up a small percentage of the world's population. The Global South is home to over 6 billion people, while the Global North has a population of just 1.6 billion.

QUIZ TIME
Official China geography

China has 34 provincial-level regions, including 23 provinces, four municipalities, five ethnic autonomous regions, and two special administrative regions.

But many people, especially anti-China pundits, politicians and propagandists, wouldn't have a clue where the places they are constantly obsessing over are even located.

Do you? Below is an official map of the People's Republic of China. Which numbers correlate to which places in China that live rent free in the heads of anti-China trolls?

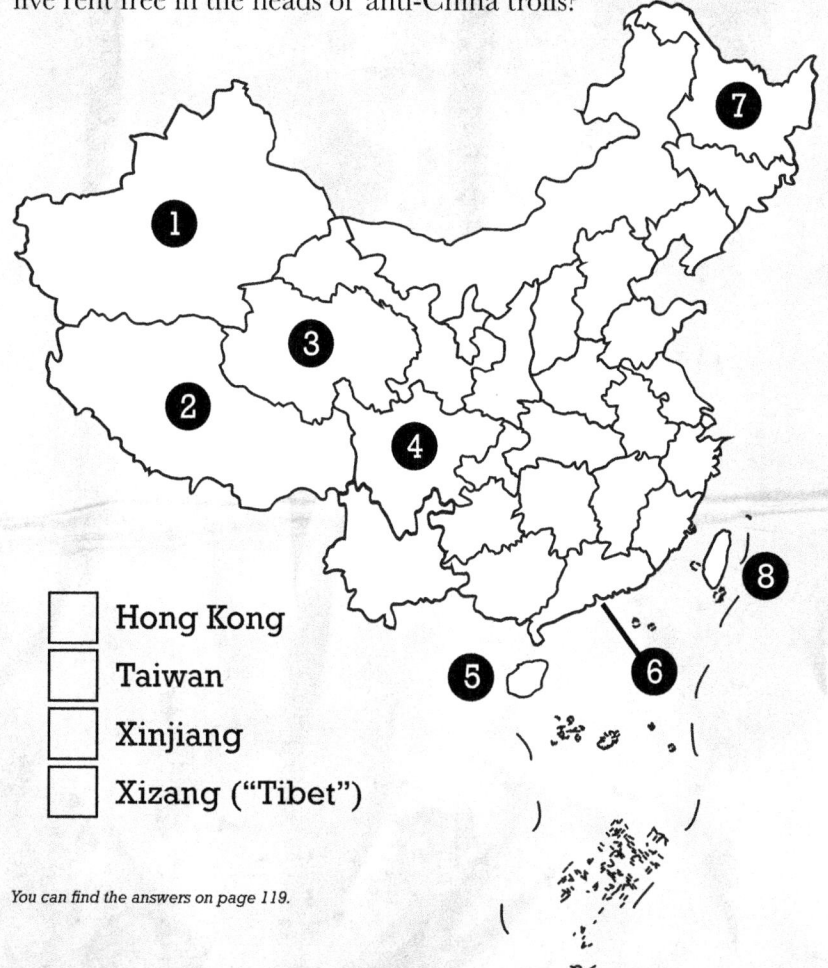

☐ Hong Kong
☐ Taiwan
☐ Xinjiang
☐ Xizang ("Tibet")

You can find the answers on page 119.

LIE #17:
YOUTUBE,
FACEBOOK, X:
BANNED
IN CHINA

The reality:

Western social media platforms are not banned in China: they were *blocked* back in 2009, and for very good reason.

China has a massive, homemade social media ecosystem that offers much more variety than in the West.

Just like in every country, social media is a popular place for Chinese citizens to share their opinions on a multitude of issues, from daily affairs to celebrity news, and yummy new restaurants to complaints about proposed new laws.

Around 78% of Chinese, or 1.1 billion people, have access to the internet,[1] making China the most connected country in the world.

Western social media apps are welcome to operate in China, but they need to follow local laws in order to do so. They refuse.

The details:

Popular Western social media platforms like YouTube, Facebook, and Twitter (now called X) were blocked in China back in 2009 after deadly riots in Xinjiang—which left 197 dead and 1,721 injured—were organized and orchestrated using those apps.

Chinese authorities requested help from the owners of Western platforms to stop riot organizers from orchestrating the citywide attacks while they were taking place, and to track down those behind the deadly attacks in the aftermath. They refused, and were subsequently blocked by China's Great Firewall.

Today, China's 1.1 billion netizens enjoy dozens upon dozens of popular local social media platforms that cater to every taste, making the widespread use of Western social media apps in China highly unnecessary.

World famous app TikTok was created right here in China. Recently, other Chinese social media platforms like 小红书

---

[1] China Internet Network Information Center (CNNIC), 2024.

(RedNote) have gained popularity in the West as well.

The legal framework

The main reason Western social media platforms like Facebook, YouTube and X are blocked in China is because their owners refuse to follow local Chinese laws that would allow them to operate here.

In short: Western platforms are more than welcome to come back to China, but they don't want to.

So which laws, particularly, are Western social media platforms not willing to follow? There are two main ones.

The first is the Measures for the Administration of Internet Information Services (State Council Decree No. 292),[1] which was enacted by China on September 25, 2000.

We'll take a look at some of the measures that relate directly to Western social media platforms operating in China.

Firstly, the law requires social media platforms operating in China to store Chinese people's user data inside the country. This is in order to protect the private data of locals users. Western social media platforms refused.

Secondly, social media companies operating in China are required to keep records for 60 days, and supply that information to authorities if requested. Western social media platforms refused.

Another requirement of social media sites under these measures is to block pornographic content. Pornography is illegal in China. Western social media platforms refused.

But one of the biggest requirements of these measures on social media sites operating inside China is the removal of any content that harms national security, unity, or social stability. Western social media platforms refused.

One clear example is the Xinjiang riots of July, 2009, largely orchestrated on Western social media platforms like Facebook,

1 中华人民共和国中央人民政府. (2000). https://www.gov.cn/gongbao/content/2000/content_60531.htm

which was a popular outlet for Uygur separatists and overseas agitators.

It would be very fair to argue that if Western social media platforms had complied with Chinese laws, the death toll of 197, as well as widespread injuries, would have been much lower.

The second piece of Chinese law that Western social media platforms refuse to follow is the 2017 Cybersecurity Law, which further details requirements of social media companies operating in China to store local users' data locally.

Article 37 states: "Personal information and important data collected and generated by operators of critical information infrastructure in their operations within the territory of the People's Republic of China shall be stored within the territory of the People's Republic of China." Western social media platforms refused.

Article 12 of that law stipulates that the internet cannot be used to endanger national security, promote terrorism, extremism, ethnic hatred, violence, obscene and pornographic material, among other things. That means that social media platforms are also responsible for ensuring the removal of such content. Western social media platforms refused.

Article 28 requires network operators to "provide technical support and assistance to public security organs and national security organs in their activities to safeguard national security and investigate crimes in accordance with the law." Western social media platforms refused.

Not popular in China anyway

An inconvenient fact about Western social media platforms operating in China is that they were never really that popular here anyway.

Anti-China trolls like to make out that if only platforms like

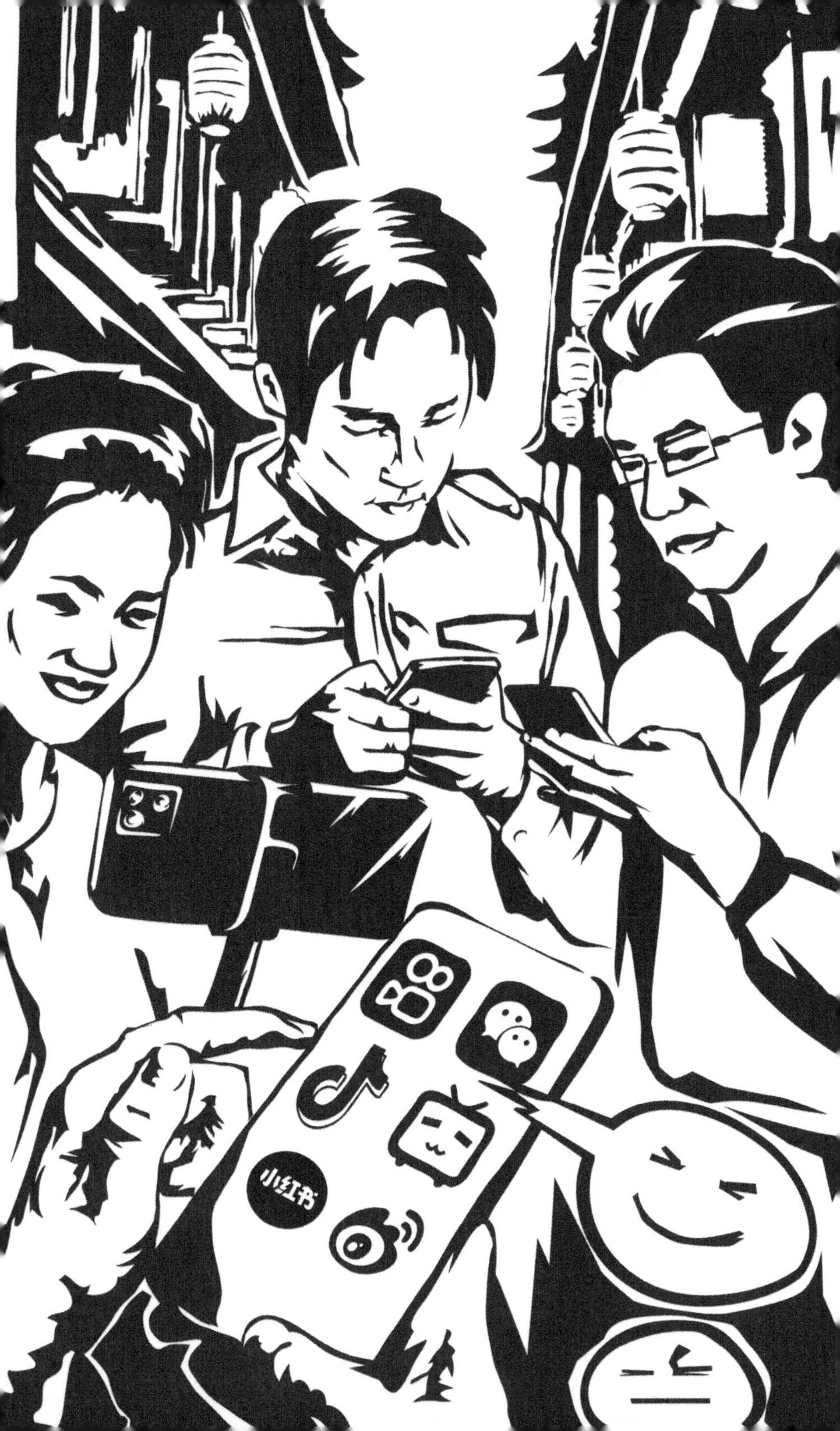
小红书

X (formerly Twitter) could open up here again, Chinese people would be somehow liberated and those apps would flourish. Not true.

Twitter operated for around three years in China, from 2006 to 2009. During that time, it was never popular and only attracted a few tens of thousands of niche users.

Local platforms at the time, like Renren, already had millions of active users. When Weibo—which many refer to as "China's Twitter"—began operating in 2009, it quickly attracted tens of millions of users as well.

This is because Twitter never had a local version of their platform, so it was hard to navigate for many Chinese users who prefer local social media that is tailored to their wants and needs, not least of all when it comes to language and content.

YouTube went live worldwide in February, 2005, including in China, but only attracted a small userbase. China created its own video sharing platform, Tudou, which was launched just a few months after YouTube and attracted millions of Chinese users.

And then on December 21, 2006, China's local video sharing platform, Youku, was launched, which was also popular locally.

YouTube, which was in English and not tailored to the needs of Chinese users, could not compete and never attracted a sizeable userbase during its short stint in the country.

Contrary to popular belief, the majority of Chinese netizens are not interested in using foreign social media platforms, instead preferring to use local social media that is specifically tailored to their unique needs and interests.

China's social media landscape

China has a vast and varied social media landscape, with dozens and dozens of different platforms either wildly popular across the population, or popular among certain subsets.

The top five Chinese social media sites based on the number of monthly active users are WeChat, with 1.34 billion[1] monthly active users; Douyin (China's version of TikTok), with 780+ million monthly active users; Kuaishou, with 680+ million monthly active users; Weibo, with 590+ million monthly active users; and Xiaohongshu (known as RedNote in the West), with 320+ million monthly active users.

Banned versus blocked

There is an important distinction between the words 'banned' and 'blocked' as it relates to Western social media usage in China.

The use of these platforms in China is not illegal because their usage is not banned. The sites are simply blocked, making it harder for Chinese netizens to use them in any great number.

In fact, Western social media apps are still used within China by a small number of people across different sectors. As just one example, many Chinese news media outlets operate YouTube, Facebook and X channels on a daily basis.

Foreigners living in China also like to use Western social media to keep in touch with friends and family back home.

So do thousands of Chinese companies whose customers are largely based outside of China. Have you heard of the Chinese Internet celebrity Tony from LC Sign? He went viral recently for his funny TikTok and Instagram videos promoting the signage company he works for. Tony and LC Sign are based in Guangdong province in southern China, and they use Western social media platforms on a daily basis.

Most anti-China trolls will argue that Western social media platforms are banned in China, implying that simply using them is illegal. That is not accurate.

---

1 This number is supplied by Tencent, the owners of WeChat, although it seems to conflict with the official count of 1.1 billion internet users in China. The higher number might account for multiple accounts.

LIE #18: CHINA IS NOT DEMOCRATIC

The reality:

China has its own system of democracy called Whole-Process People's Democracy which is, in many ways, much more democratic than Western electoral democracies.

Whole-Process People's Democracy

China's system of Whole-Process People's Democracy allows the people of China to take part in the democratic process throughout each and every step, and not just by voting once every three or four years during an election cycle of empty promises and scandal.

President Xi Jinping once described Western style electoral democracy this way: "If the people merely have the right to vote but no right of extensive participation, in other words, if they are awakened only at election time but go into hibernation afterwards, this is token democracy."[1]

The extensive participation President Xi is talking about includes elections, consultation, a nationwide system of representative people's congresses, multiparty cooperation, regional ethnic autonomy, and public oversight. All of these are aspects of China's unique form of democracy.

Elections

Contrary to popular belief, there are elections held regularly in China, across many different areas, but they are somewhat different from the Western style.

As opposed to the West, where people vote for their leaders (the United States) or for the political party of their choice (New Zealand) in often dramatic and scandal-laden election campaigns, Chinese citizens vote for their representatives at the urban and rural grassroots level.[2]

---

[1] Li, Junru. (2023). Chinese-Style Democracy: Whole-Process People's Democracy. Page 86.
[2] Chen, Jian. (2019). Contemporary China's Politics. Page 240.

"Elections in China are extensive and cover all aspects of the country's political and social life. They include elections to government institutions, villagers and urban residents committees, and employees congresses in enterprises and public institutions."[1]

China's political appointment system is quite hierarchical in nature, with the role of president right at the very top. No person can normally become a leader in China without having slowly made their way up the ladder, often from village or urban neighborhood level, all the way to higher and higher positions like city and provincial level roles.

President Xi's path to top leadership took four decades. Along the way he had many roles across the government and the party, including Deputy Party Secretary of a county, vice mayor of a city, Party Secretary of a prefecture, Deputy Party Secretary of a province, acting governor of a province, Party Secretary of Shanghai, and Vice President of China.

In China, public elections are held to vote in representatives at the lowest levels of governance. In urban areas, that might include village or town committees who take charge of local affairs. In urban areas, residents also vote for their neighborhood committees, who are officially at the same level as village committees.

After that, representatives are then able to climb the ranks over decades of hard work and proving their abilities. Elections in China are, in a way, an escalator allowing people who want to devote their careers to the country to get on at the ground floor.

Consultation

Public consultation is a major aspect of Chinese democracy, whereby governments at all levels across the country ensure that "the people participate in the management of state affairs, social affairs, and economic and cultural affairs," as well as soliciting "opinions and suggestions," not only at the local level, but also at

---

[1] State Council Information Office of the People's Republic of China. (2021). China: Democracy That Works. Page 22.

the highest level.[1]

All governments are required to regularly consult with the public, seeking their feedback on everything from proposed laws, right through to how they're enforced.

Consultation also occurs between governments and members of the public across every sector of society, from ordinary people to specialized experts, and ethnic minorities to religious figures.

One of the main forms of consultation is undertaken through China's vast network of people's congresses, which provide a representative group of citizens from all walks of life the opportunity to take part in political consultation, democratic supervision, and participation in government and state affairs.[2]

Deputies to people's congresses are elected directly by the public at the lowest levels, township and county. From then on, people's congresses at higher levels are elected from the level below.

Those deputies are fully representative of the people. "They come from all regions, ethnic groups, sectors and social groups, and function at national, provincial, city, county and township levels. At the end of 2020, 2.62 million people were serving as deputies to people's congresses at all levels nationwide."[3]

There are also regular opportunities for members of the public to meet with their representatives and ask them questions and so on. In Shanghai, for example, every neighborhood has set days every week for local representatives to meet directly with the public for consultation.

"Making full use of their close connections with the people, these deputies diligently fulfill their duties by soliciting and submitting people's suggestions and advice through various forms and channels."[4]

Apart from that, there are many other forms of consultation between the government and the public, via many different

---

[1] Li, Junru. (2023). Chinese-Style Democracy: Whole-Process People's Democracy. Page 87.
[2] Chen, Jian. (2019). Contemporary China's Politics. Page 44.
[3] State Council Information Office of the People's Republic of China. (2021). China: Democracy That Works. Page 11.
[4] Same as above.

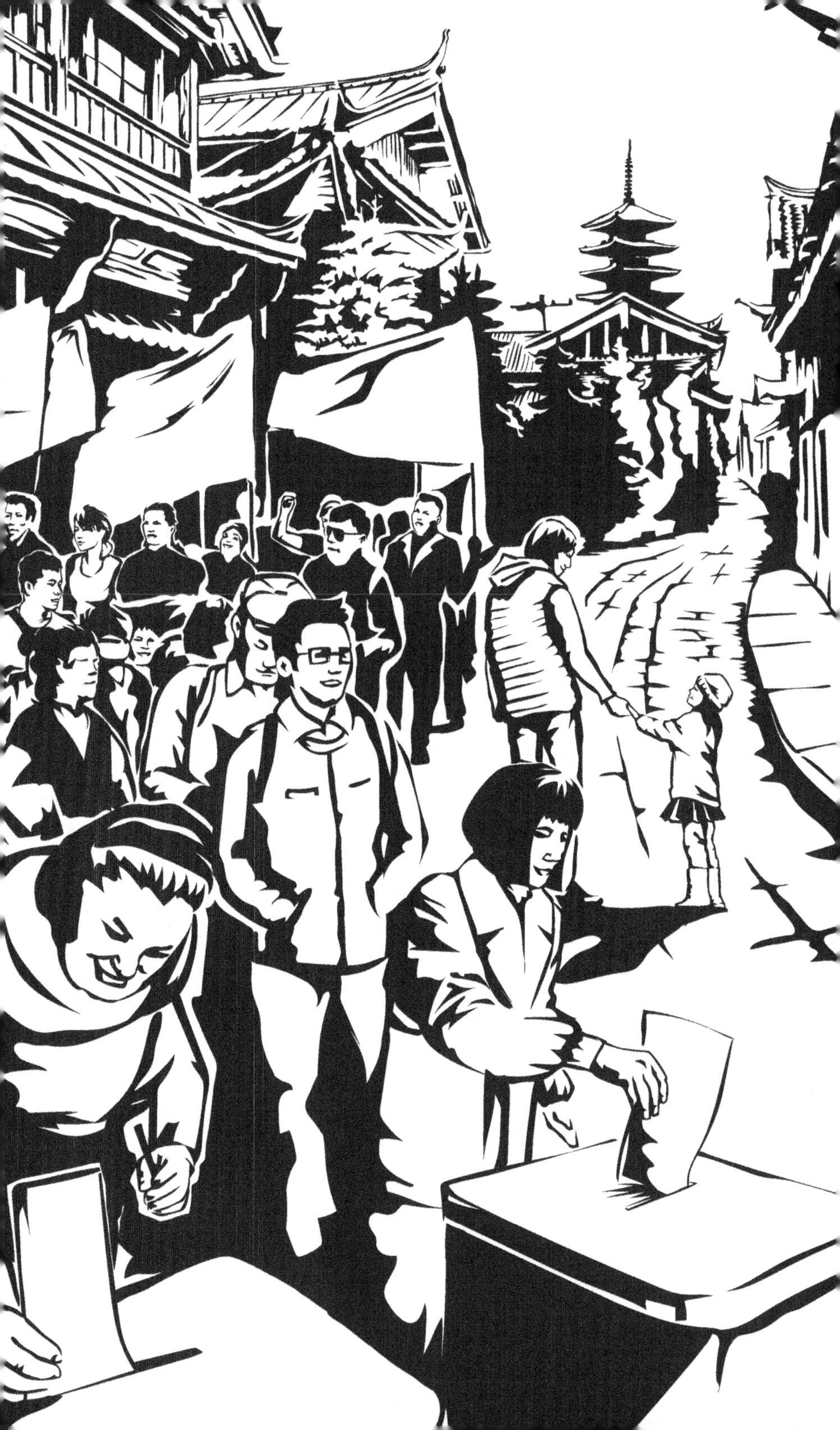

channels that include proposals, seminars, public meetings and conferences, the internet, and opinion polls.

These forms of public consultation might be wide, or highly targeted, depending on the situation. "On matters that have a bearing on the interests of everyone, extensive consultations will be held throughout the whole of society; on matters that concern the interests of people in one specific region, consultations will be held locally; on matters that affect the interests of a certain group, consultations will be held among those groups; and on matters that concern the interests of a community, consultations will be held with the community."[1]

Ethnic autonomy

One of the most unique aspects of Chinese democracy is regional ethnic autonomy, where certain geographical areas across China that are home to large concentrations of ethnic minorities are governed by those people.

Ethnic autonomous areas come in many sizes, such as prefectures and counties, which may have a few thousand residents, all the way up to provincial-level regions which are home to millions, of which China has five. They include the Xinjiang Uygur Autonomous Region and the Xizang ("Tibet") Autonomous Region.

There are 155 ethnic autonomous areas in China, and all are governed by the people of that area's ethnic groups. "On all standing committees of people's congresses of the 155 ethnic autonomous areas, there are citizens from the local ethnic groups assuming the office of chair or vice chair; all governors, prefectural commissioners, and heads of counties of ethnic autonomous areas are citizens from the ethnic group."[2]

Of the 55 ethnic minorities in China, 44 have their own autonomous areas established, which makes up the majority (71%) of people from ethnic minorities in the country.[3]

1 State Council Information Office of the People's Republic of China. (2021). China: Democracy That Works. Page 25.
2 State Council Information Office of the People's Republic of China. (2021). China: Democracy That Works. Page 18.
3 Zheng, Qian. (2010). China's Ethnic Groups and Religions. Page 70.

Multi-party cooperation

Many people believe China has only one political party, the CPC. In actual fact, a key aspect of China's political system is multi-party cooperation. There are nine political parties in China —including the CPC—all of whom play an active role in decision making.

For example, each political party is represented at the Chinese People's Political Consultative Conference (CPPCC), an important body elected every five years to discuss China's direction. The majority of the CPPCC's members are not members of the Communist Party of China,[1] and this is a legal requirement.

Unlike Western-style liberal democracies, China does not have opposition parties and any of the conflict that goes with that system. Instead, the different political parties in China work together constructively. Their work includes taking part in "the formulation and implementation of ... national policies, principles, laws and regulations, and participate in the administration of ... national political power and state affairs."[2]

Chinese see China as very democratic

China is among the highest scoring countries in the world when it comes to citizens believing their country is actually democratic – 79% of Chinese think so, according to the Democracy Perception Index 2024. The same report also found that "public perceptions of government accountability remain among the world's highest in China."

Surprisingly, the authors of the index continue to refer to China as "non-democratic," despite the vast majority of Chinese people saying their country is democratic, and the vast majority of Western respondents believing their countries are *not* democratic.

That's very undemocratic of the authors, don't you think?

---
[1] Chen, Jian. (2019). Contemporary China's Politics. Page 47.
[2] Same as above. Page 41.

A 2021 white paper by China's State Council Information Office put it succinctly: "Whether a country is democratic should be judged by its people, not dictated by a handful of outsiders."

As Xi Jinping once said: "There is no uniform or single model of democracy; it comes in many forms. Assessing the world's myriad political systems against a single yardstick and examining diverse political advancement in monochrome is, [in] itself, inherently undemocratic."[1]

Touché!

EXTRA FACTS

★ In 2016 and 2017, more than 900 million voters took part in the election of deputies to people's congresses, the world's largest direct elections.

★ Voting in China is open to all citizens of the People's Republic of China who are 18 or over, unless they have been deprived of political rights according to the law.

★ The Communist Party of China's key slogan is 为人民服务, To Serve The People, which highlights its desire for governance in the interests of the people.

★ Regional ethnic autonomy was written into the first Constitution of the PRC way back in 1954, making it one of China's core political systems.

---

1 Speech by Xi Jinping at the Central People's Work Conference (October 2021)

GAMES ANSWER PAGE

Thanks for playing along! Here are the answers to the quizzes from this handbook.

Anti-China lies crossword

1: TAIWAN. 2: WUMAO. 3: RELIGIONS. 4: BRAINWASH. 5: DEMOCRACY. 6: WINNIE. 7: GENOCIDE. 8: XIZANG. 9: SOCIALCREDIT. 10: FENTANYL.

"CHINA THREAT" AI BATTLE

The first essay was written by China's DeepSeek, while the second was written by Elon Musk's Grok.

Half-time exam

1: B. 2: B. 3: B. 4: B.

Official China geography

Hong Kong: 6. Taiwan: 8. Xinjiang: 1. Xizang: 2.

ONE MORE TEST!

Just to make sure you've got it committed to memory, write the Chinese characters for *wumao* below.

LIE #19:
CHINA WANTS TO SPREAD COMMUNISM

The reality:

China has no plans—or even any desire—to export its system of governance around the world, be it communism, socialism, or any other model. One of China's core principles when it comes to international relations is non-interference and the respect of sovereignty.

The details:

China is well aware that its system of governance is best suited to its own, unique culture, history, and path. With that in mind, Beijing is absolutely not interested in exporting communism or any other form of Chinese governance around the world.

The government of China believes that every country needs to follow its own path, and find a system of governance that fits uniquely with that country and its people.

Socialism with Chinese Characteristics

One of China's core governance principles and ideologies is Socialism with Chinese Characteristics, which is a system of socialist democracy based on China's unique circumstances. China knows that this system would not and could not work if directly transplanted onto another country.

The term was created under Deng Xiaoping and first formalized in 1982 at the 12th National Congress, which ultimately allowed China's unique and unprecedented foray into reform and opening up. Basically, it allowed some capitalist ideas to make sense inside the boundaries of its socialist democracy.

Reform and opening up, which began in 1979, allowed China to improve living standards, reduce inequality, and ensure social stability. Since then, China has lifted over 800 million people out of poverty. Recently, President Xi introduced Socialism with Chinese Characteristics in the New Era, which introduced new aspects including anti-corruption campaigns, poverty alleviation, and projects like the Belt and Road Initiative.

Non-interference in other countries

One of China's core principles when it comes to international relations is non-interference in the domestic affairs of other states.

Such an approach is completely unlike Western nations, who cannot help but to constantly interfere in China's affairs, pressuring Beijing to do this or that, and even threatening to punish China based on their own political and social preferences.

This policy comes from China's Five Principles of Peaceful Coexistence—mutual respect for sovereignty, territorial integrity, non-aggression, non-interference, and equality—which were articulated way back in 1954.

China pushes for each nation to have the right to determine its own political, economic and social systems without external pressure, and it hopes for the same courtesy in return.

EXTRA FACTS:

★China's unique form of governance includes Confucian values like social harmony and collective welfare, blending them with Marxism to create a distinctly Chinese socialism that emphasizes stability and national pride.

★Some states draw inspiration from China's model: Ethiopia and Rwanda have studied China's state-led development, though Beijing actively avoids pushing ideological conversion.

★China's Five Principles for Peaceful Coexistence were first formalized in a 1954 agreement between China and India, between Chinese Premier Zhou Enlai and Indian Prime Minister Jawaharlal Nehru, during talks to guide bilateral relations.

LIE #20: CHINA IS BAD FOR THE PLANET

The reality:

China is going above and beyond all other countries in the world to make the planet greener and reduce pollution. In fact, many of China's laws make it a legal requirement that the development and management of the country is done with the environment in mind.

The details:

Many Westerners have this idea in their mind, when they think of China, of mass pollution and gray skies. While that image was a reality even up to 10 or 15 years ago in many places, China has made massive strides in reducing carbon emissions, and helping make not just China greener, but the entire world.

For example, China is now the world's largest producer of solar and wind energy. By 2024, it also accounted for over 40% of global solar panel production and installed more than 400 gigawatts of wind and solar capacity. China exceeds the U.S. in solar and wind energy production, with over three times the installed capacity and double the energy output.

On top of that, China leads the world in the production and uptake of electric vehicles, selling over 8 million EVs in 2023 alone. China's government is helping the move to electric vehicles with infrastructure support: as of October 2024, China had approximately 3.4 million public EV charging points, with 1.5 million of those being fast chargers.

When it comes to afforestation, China is again ahead of the curve. In 2024, China planted 4.45 million hectares of trees[1] (approximately 13.35 billion trees), more than any other country in the world by far. And that race to greenify the country will not slow down any time soon, because China's government has pledged to plant 70 billion trees by the year 2030, in support of the Paris Agreement.[2]

---

1 https://news.cgtn.com/news/2025-01-26/China-plants-4-45-million-hectares-of-trees-in-2024-1Au5tsCXvbi/p.html
2 https://www.weforum.org/press/2022/05/china-will-aim-to-plant-and-conserve-70-billion-trees-by-2030-as-part-of-the-global-tree-movement/

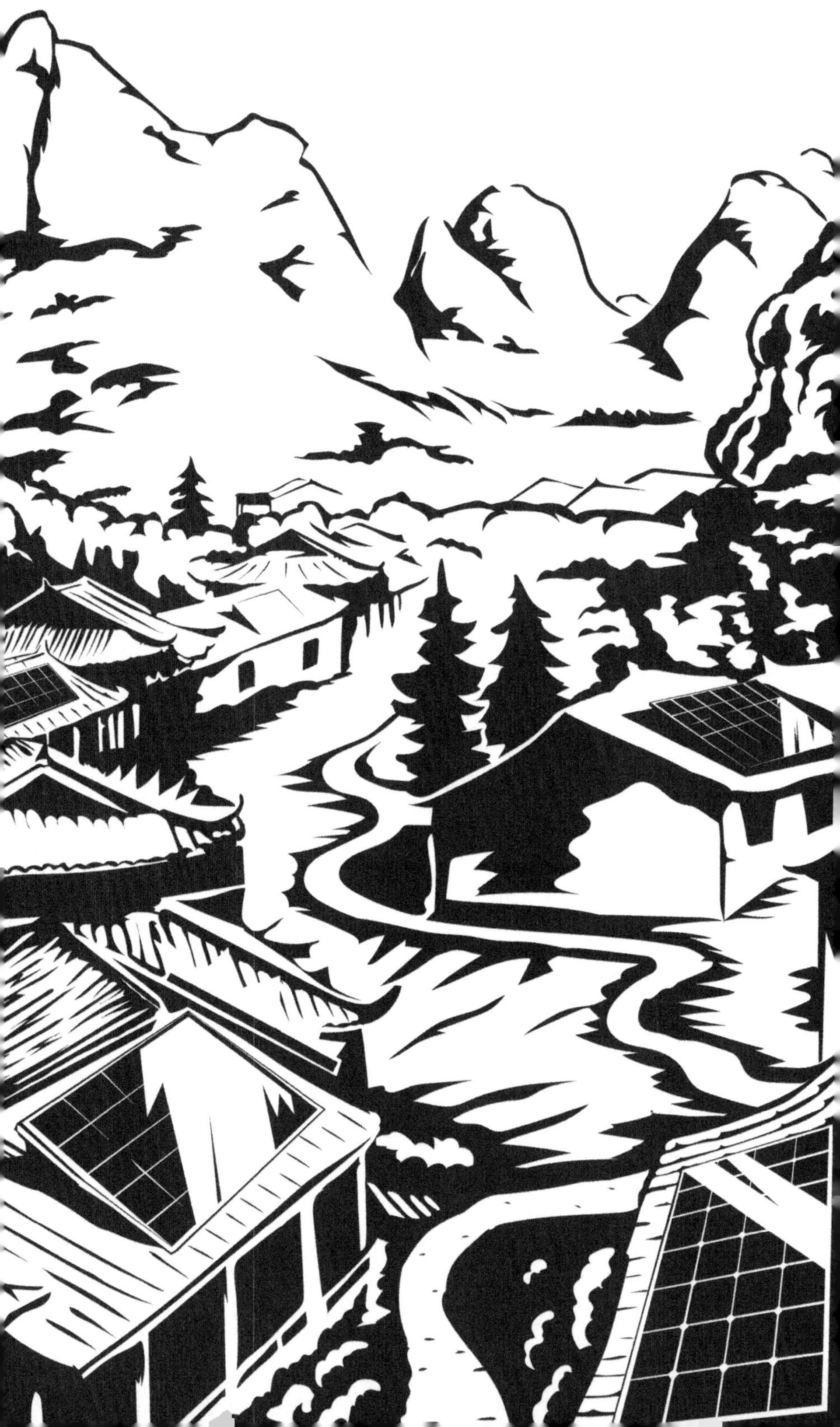

Government greening

So how is it that China is so successful in its green initiatives? Well, it all comes down to support from the top.

The Chinese government places massive importance on reducing carbon emissions and making the world a greener place, and has written environmental goals directly into its medium and long-term plans for the country.[1]

That not only means the creation of relevant laws and policies, but also ensures government support in its realization.

Carbon neutrality

One of China's most important goals when it comes to the environment is its aim to achieve carbon neutrality by the year 2060. That means that by then, China will offset all of its own carbon emissions.

China has another significant goal, which is to achieve peak carbon emissions by the year 2030. That means that China's annual emissions after that year will be lower and lower.

As with many of its other targets, China will most likely reach these two milestones ahead of time.

EXTRA FACTS:

★Environmental protection has been written into China's plans ever since the beginning of the PRC: in the first Five-Year Plan (1953–1957), policies included afforestation, soil and water conversion, comprehensive use of waste materials, and "patriotic" public health campaigns.[2]

★In line with its Construction of a Community of Shared Future, China aims to lead the world in environmental protection, while making green technology and its implementation accessible,

---

1 Zhang, Haibin. (2022). China and Global Climate Governance. Page 100.
2 Duan, Juan. (2010). Ecological Civilization of Contemporary China. Page 10.

even for the poorest nations.

★Completed in 2025, the Taklamakan Green Barrier is a 3,046 kilometer-long vegetation belt that encircles China's largest desert, the Taklamakan Desert located in Xinjiang.

★China's forest growth from 2001–2021 was more than the next 19 countries combined, according to World Bank data.

★Over 11,800 protected areas cover 18% of China's land, aiding species like the giant panda, downgraded from endangered to vulnerable.

★While China's carbon emissions are quite high if you look at the total when compared to other countries, China's per capita emissions are moderate. The highest carbon emissions per capita come from oil producing nations, followed by Western countries like the United States and Australia.

THE END

Thank you for making it to the very end of the *Wumao Handbook Vol. 1*! I hope the information provided in this book truly helps you to not only re-educate the anti-China trolls in your life, but that it also gave *you* some new insights into this fascinating and complex country that I have called home for the past decade.

The *Wumao Handbook Vol. 2* is already in the works, with anti-China lies around Xinjiang genocide, Chinese media brainwashing, the South China Sea, protest in China, and more!

Having read the first volume, I would love to hear your thoughts and feedback. What did you enjoy about this handbook? What could I improve for next time? You can let me know via my website, **reportsonchina.com** or on X (Twitter): @AndyBxxx.

Also, don't forget to check out my YouTube channel, Reports on China, where I post new videos every few days.

Thanks again, and I'll see you all next time!

PS: The link is *YouTube.com/ReportsOnChina*

BIBLIOGRAPHY

Chen, Han-seng. (1949). *Frontier Land Systems in Southwest China.*

Chen, Jian. (2019). *Contemporary China's Politics.*

Deshayes, Laurent. (1997). *Histoire du Tibet, Librairie Arthème Fayard.*

Duan, Juan. (2010). *Ecological Civilization of Contemporary China.*

Ettinger, Albert. (2018). *Free Tibet? Power, society, and ideology in old Tibet.*

Kawaguchi, Enai. (1909). *Three Years in Tibet.*

Li, Junru. (2023). *Chinese-Style Democracy: Whole-Process People's Democracy.*

Lin, Jianhua. (2022). *China's Whole-Process People's Democracy.*

Party School of the CPC Central Committee Press. (2001). *Opinions of Three Generations of CPC Leaders on the Taiwan Question, Chin. ed.*

Ruan, Qing. (2021). *All For The People.*

State Council Information Office of the People's Republic of China. (2020). *White Papers of the State Council Information Office on Xinjiang (2003 - 2019).*

State Council Information Office of the People's Republic of China. (2021). *China: Democracy That Works.*

State Council Information Office of the People's Republic of China. (2025). *Controlling Fentanyl-Related Substances—China's Contribution.*

State Council Information Office, the People's Republic of China. (2025). *Human Rights in Xizang in the New Era.*

The Institute of Contemporary China Studies. (2019). *A Concise History of the People's Republic of China (1949-2019).*

The Taiwan Affairs Office of the State Council and The State Council Information Office. (2022). *White Paper: The Taiwan Question and China's Reunification in the New Era.*

Xinhua Publishing House. (2023). *China Yearbook 2023 (volume 38).*

Ye, Xiaowen. (2018). *Pluralism and Harmony in the Religions of China.*

Zhang, Haibin. (2022). *China and Global Climate Governance.*

Zheng, Qian. (2010). *China's Ethnic Groups and Religions.*

INDEX

5G 53, 57
1992 Consensus 73
2008 financial crisis 53
2017 Cybersecurity Law 106

A

Afforestation 126, 128
Alibaba 77
Alipay 80
America's Food and Drug Administration 43
Apple 86
Artificial Intelligence 52
Asia 44, 53, 56, 58, 77, 100
Australia 16, 84, 100, 129
Australian Strategic Policy Institute (ASPI) 85, 86

B

Beijing 14-18, 32, 33, 69, 73, 77, 90, 122, 123
Beiting Command and Pacification Commissioner's Office 63
Belgium 44
Belt and Road Initiative 53, 56, 62, 123
Bible 25
Bishkek 64
Bloom, Orlando 70
British Council 58
Buddhism 22, 25, 71
Buddhist Association of China 23
Budweiser 77
Burger King 86
But at what cost? 101

C

Canada 16, 42, 48
Canceled With Chinese Characteristics 76, 77
Carbon emissions 126, 128, 129
Carbon neutrality 128
Catholicism 23, 25, 73
Chiang Ching-kuo 17
Chiang Kai-shek 17
China Bird Project 96

China Buddhist Association 25
China Christian Council 25
China Islamic Association 25
China Patriotic Catholic Association 25
China's Great Firewall 104
China Taoist Association 25
China Threat 7, 9, 52-58
Chinese government 27, 32, 43, 61, 77, 101, 128
Chinese mainland 14, 15, 17, 91
Chinese People's Political Consultative Conference 25, 117
CIA 65
Civil War 16, 17
Communism 7, 122
Communist Party of China (CPC) 10, 17, 55, 57, 91, 117
Confucianism 25, 73
Confucius Institute 54
Constitution of the People's Republic of China 24, 32
Constitution of the Republic of China 15
Construction of a Community of Shared Future 128
Consultation 113, 114
Convention Against Illicit Traffic 43
Counter-terrorism 48
COVID 101
Cultural genocide 33
Cultural Revolution 23

D

Dalai Lama 68, 71, 73
Dao 23
Debt-trap diplomacy 53
DeepSeek 51, 52, 59, 119
Degeneres, Ellen 76
Democracy 28, 92, 93, 112, 113, 116, 118, 122
Democracy Perception Index 100, 117
Democratic Progressive Party (DPP) 18, 19
Deng, Xiaoping 90, 91, 122
Disappear 75, 76
Djibouti 57, 59
Douyin 109
Drepung monastery 69

E

East Turkistan 63, 64

East Turkistan Islamic Movement (ETIM) 63
East Turkistan Islamic Republic 63, 64
Edelman Trust Barometer 27, 28
Egypt 100
Elections 112, 113
Electric vehicles (EVs) 126
Ethiopia 123
Ettinger, Albert 69, 70, 71
Europe 44, 53, 56, 100

F

Facebook 7, 64, 93, 104, 105, 109
Fan, Bingbing 77
Fentanyl 41-44
Fifty Cent Army 10
Five Principles of Peaceful Coexistence 123
Five-Year Plan 128
France 16
Free Tibet 7, 68-71
Fudan University 11
Fujian Province 19

G

General Zheng Chenggong 18
Genocide 33, 130
Gere, Richard 70
Germany 16, 84
Global North 100
Global South 100
Goldman, David P. 53
Green technology 128
Grok 51, 52, 59, 119
Gulf of Aden 59

H

Hami Garrison Command 63
Han Chinese 33, 34, 62, 70
Harvard University 27, 28
Hilton 86
Hilton, Paris 68, 70
Hollywood 68, 70, 76
Homicide 48

Hong Kong 15, 19, 91-93, 100, 119
Huawei 53
Hugo Boss 77
Hu, Jintao 91

I
India 22, 123
Indo-Pacific 58
Islam 23, 25, 73
Israel 16

J
James, Jaq 86
Japan 16, 27, 28, 84, 100
Jiang, Zemin 91

K
Kawaguchi, Enai 70
Kazak 34, 62
Kenya 56, 100
KFC 86
Kirgiz 34, 62
Koran 23
Kuaishou 109
Kunming Railway Station 48, 63
Kuomintang (KMT) 17, 18
Kyrgyzstan 64

L
Languages 7, 23, 31-34, 90
Latin America 44, 100
Laurence Austine Waddell 70
LC Sign 109
Lhasa 69, 70
Liuqiu 18
Li, Yifeng 77

M
Ma, Jack 77
Macau 15, 91, 92
Mahbubani, Kishore 53
Mandarin 10, 11, 33, 34, 39, 86

Mao, Zedong 17, 90
Marriott 86
Marxism 123
McDonald's 86
Measures for the Administration of Internet Information Services 105
Ming Dynasty 63
Minority languages 32, 34
Mongolian 34, 62
Multi-party cooperation 117

N
National Endowment for Democracy (NED) 9, 65
National People's Congress 25
Nehru, Jawaharlal 123
New Zealand 11, 16, 112
New Zealand Film School 11
Nike 86
No First Use 59
Non-aggression 123
Non-interference 53, 59, 122, 123
North America 44

O
One China principle 15, 73, 91
One Country, Two Systems 73, 90-92

P
Panda 129
Paris Agreement 126
Peak carbon emissions 128
Peng, Shuai 77
People's Republic of China 14, 17, 19, 23, 24, 32, 64, 84, 90, 106, 118
Pepsi-Cola 77
Philippines 56, 100
Pitt, Brad 68, 70
Pivot to Asia 58
Pollution 126
Pornography 105
Prada 77
Prime Minister of New Zealand 11
Professor Du Ruiqing 54
Protestantism 23

Q
Qing Dynasty 63

R
RedNote 104, 109
Regional ethnic autonomy 112, 116
Religion 7, 21, 24
Renren 108
Reports on China 4, 10
Republic of East Turkistan 63
Resolution 2758 16
Respect for sovereignty 123
Reunification 90-92
Ross, John 52
Russians 62
Rwanda 123

S
Saudi Arabia 58
Seaboard Geographic Gazetteer 18
Seagal, Steven 68, 70
Serfs 68, 69
Shanghai 33, 39, 45, 73, 113, 114
Shanghai Disneyland 39, 45, 73
Shanghainese 33
Shen Ying 18
Single Convention on Narcotic Drugs 43
Sino-Vietnam war 59
Skechers 85
Slave labor 7, 9, 83-85
Social Credit Score 7, 9, 79, 80
Socialism 59, 122, 123
Socialism with Chinese Characteristics 59, 122
Social media 64, 103-106, 108, 109
Song Dynasty 18
South Africa 100
South China Sea 15, 56, 57, 130
Southeast Asia 77
South Korea 100
Special Administrative Region (SAR) 92
Starbucks 86
State of Wu 18

Statista 27, 28
Sui Dynasty 18
Switzerland 100

T
Taipei 14-18
Taiwan 13, 89, 119
Taiwan Strait 14
Taklamakan Desert 129
Taklamakan Green Barrier 129
Taobao 49
Taoism 23
Territorial integrity 57, 123
Three Kingdoms Period 18
Tibet 7, 19, 25, 32, 34, 67-71, 93, 116
Tibetan language 32, 33
TikTok 104, 109
Tony from LC Sign 109
To Serve The People 118
Trump, Donald 42
Tudou 108
Twitter 11, 64, 104, 108

U
Ukraine 100
United Kingdom 16, 27, 28
United Nations 16
United States 9, 23, 27, 28, 42, 43, 48, 53, 54, 56, 57, 58, 62, 64, 84, 85, 100, 101, 126
United States Congress 9
UN Security Council 59
U.S. Agency for Global Media 9
USAID 9
Uyghur Forced Labor Prevention Act 84
Uyghur Rights Advocacy Project 65
Uygur 7, 32-34, 62-65, 83-86, 106, 116

V
Vatican City 15
Victoria University 11
Vietnam 56, 59

W

Washington, DC 9, 62, 64, 65, 86
WeChat 80, 109
Weibo 108, 109
Wellington 11
Western Han Dynasty 62
Western Regions 62, 63
Whole-Process People's Democracy 112, 114
Winnie the Pooh 7, 9, 37, 39, 45, 73
World Bank 129
World Uyghur Congress 65
WTO 54
Wu, Kris 77

X

X (formerly Twitter) 7, 93, 103-105, 108, 109
Xibe 62
Xi, Jinping 25, 91, 112, 118
Xinjiang Papers 85
Xinjiang riots 105
Xinjiang Uygur Autonomous Region 7, 19, 29, 32-34, 61-65, 83-87, 93, 96, 104, 105, 116, 119, 129, 130
Xizang Autonomous Region 19, 25, 32-34, 67-72, 116, 119

Y

Youku 108
YouTube 103-105, 108
Yuan dynasty 18, 63
Yuan Dynasty 63
Yunnan University 63

Z

Zenz, Adrian 85, 86
Zheng, Chenggong 18
Zhou, Enlai 123
Zhuang 34

Printed in Great Britain
by Amazon